MILTON

MILTON

A COMPENDIUM

Anthony Mitchell Sammarco

Charleston   London

THE
History
PRESS

Published by The History Press
Charleston, SC 29403
www.historypress.net

Copyright © 2010 by Anthony Mitchell Sammarco
All rights reserved

Images are from the collection of the Milton Historical Society, unless otherwise credited.

First published 2010

Manufactured in the United States

ISBN 978.1.59629.377.9

Library of Congress Cataloging-in-Publication Data

Sammarco, Anthony Mitchell.
Milton : a compendium / Anthony Mitchell Sammarco.
p. cm.
ISBN 978-1-59629-377-9
1. Milton (Mass. : Town)--History. 2. Milton (Mass. : Town)--Biography. I. Title.
F74.M66S27 2010
974.4'7--dc22
2010036874

In honor of Patricia Desmond, Editor of the Milton Times

CONTENTS

ACKNOWLEDGEMENTS

O ver the last decade, many people have assisted in the suggestion, researching and writing of these articles, which appeared in the *Milton Times*. Patricia Desmond, publisher of the newspaper, encouraged me to write these glimpses into the history and development of Milton, Massachusetts. Over many years, people expressed their continued interest, and I asked Pat if I might publish a selection of them in book format. This book is the result of that decade-long association and friendship, and I dedicate this book to her.

I would also like to thank: Donald and Cynthia Agnetta; the late Grace Badger; Eddie Baker; Bayou Bend, Museum of Fine Arts, Houston, Texas; the Boston Athenaeum; Helen Buchanan; the late Paul G. Buchanan; Henry Carr; Rosamond Whitney Carr; Joe Cedrone; Enid Chapman; Janet Christiansen; Elise Ciregna and Stephen Lo Piccolo; Edith Clifford; Mary Cobb; Edith Cunningham Crocker; the late Martha T. Curtis; Elizabeth Curtiss; Annie Davis and Frank Schroth; Margaret Dillon; William Dillon; Brian Doherty; Paul Dolan; Kevin Donahue; Mike Doyle; Jean Dudley; Edward Duffy; Olivia Grant Dybing; Libby and Fred Eustis; William Fall; First Parish Church, Unitarian; Tally Saltonstall Forbes; Mary and Frank Furber; Eleanor Fusoni; Edward Gordon; Daniel Haacker; Helen Hannon; the late Joanna Henry; the late Virginia Holbrook; the Viscount Hood of Whitley; the late William Morris Hunt; Hutchinson; Donna and Peter Jackson; Dr. and Mrs. David Jackson; Marjorie Shaw Jeffries; Richard Kenworthy;

Kidder Peabody & Company; the late William Laughran; Nadine Leary; Paul Leo; Robert Mason; Judith McGillicuddy; Milton Cemetery; Milton Hospital; Sylvia Mitchell; Elizabeth Mock; Hilda Morrill; Don and Emma Jean Moulton; James Mullen, Milton town clerk; Ellen Ochs; Stephen O'Donnell; James Pardy; the late Jeannette Peverly; Daniel Pierce; Linda and Steve Pirie; Elva Proctor; Lilian Randall; Joseph Reardon; Margaret Recanzone; Bernadette C. Richards; Perry Russell; Jeffrey Saraceno, my editor; Carolyn Savage; Andy Sawicky; Robert Bayard Severy; Therese Desmond-Sills; Jean Pierce Stetson; Jeanne and Bill Sutton; Anne and George Thompson; Carolyn Thornton; Mary and Charles Truslow; the late Ruth Tucker; Steven Walker, South End Photo Lab; Ann and Tom Walsh; the Ware family; Ellen and Tom White; Carolyn Pierce Williams; Jack and Marie Zinkus.

INTRODUCTION

Milton, Massachusetts, is a well-placed and bucolic town located between the Neponset River and the Blue Hills Reservation. Adjacent to the city of Boston on the north, Quincy to the south and east and Canton to the west, Milton is only a few miles from Beacon Hill. It is located near Boston Harbor, to which it has water access through the Neponset River Estuary, and has sweeping panoramic views from Milton Hill. Milton is a welcoming town that embraces people from everywhere and creates a thriving nexus of people who continue to espouse Milton as the best place to live, being named in 2007 as one of the top ten places to live in the United States, according to *Money Magazine*.

Milton, Massachusetts, was settled in 1640 by Puritans who arrived from England and established Massachusetts Bay Colony in 1630. Incorporated in 1662 as an independent town from Dorchester, Massachusetts, it remains as such today, although it borders the city of Boston on the north along the Neponset River. For the first two centuries after its founding, Milton remained an agrarian community with farms and open lands, as well as industrial activity along the Neponset River at Milton Village, which included a gristmill in 1634, a gunpowder mill in 1674, a paper mill in 1728 and a chocolate mill in 1765, all of which are thought to be among the first of their kind in New England. By the mid-nineteenth century, Milton's population began to steadily increase due to the ease of transportation of the Dorchester and Milton Branch of the Old

The Hoosic-Whisick Pines were in the Scots Woods area of Milton, near the Great Blue Hill, which can be seen in the distance. Ralph Houghton (1623–1705) had a farm in the area, and it was for him that Houghton's Pond was named. Photographed in 1905 by Frederick Frizzell, this stand of pines would give its name to the golf club. *Author's collection.*

Colony Railroad, which provided railway access to Boston with a depot at Mattapan Square and passenger stations at Central Avenue and Milton Village. Today, the former railroad line is perpetuated by the surface trolley connecting Ashmont Station and Mattapan Square and has stations on both the Dorchester and Milton sides of the river. A horse-drawn streetcar began running in 1856 from the Lower Mills to Boston via Dorchester Avenue (the former turnpike), so the ease of transportation increasingly allowed people of all walks of life to live in Milton but commute to the city for business, shopping or pleasure.

In the May 12, 1883 edition of the *Milton News*, there appeared an editorial that is considered startlingly prophetic as to the rampant development that would ultimately occur in the town over the next century. It said,

> *Milton is so conveniently located near Boston that its growth as a dwelling place for people carrying on business in the metropolis is assured beyond a doubt. The only drawback to a rapid growth is the manifest desire of many land owners to keep their property out of the market and thereby preserve the antiquity of its topography…A truly good man will not monopolize all the eligible real estate for his own gratification alone, it will be either for the purpose of doing some good, real or imaginary to the community or town, or a combination of circumstances may draw him to withhold it for a better end.*

By the mid-nineteenth century, Milton was no longer a rural farming town. Located just seven miles from Boston, the town had thriving commercial concerns along the Neponset River and businesses at Milton Village and East Milton. The Granite Railway Company had, since its inception in 1826, provided quarried granite for a multitude of purposes and could boast of being the first railway in the United States. From what was once a primarily agrarian community, Milton had by 1865 attracted many families that purchased the former farms to create gentlemen's estates that dotted the town. These new residents were to create a network of families and friends that sought to retain the rural character of Milton, but by the early twentieth century, rampant development was taking place on all sides—in Dorchester, Mattapan and Hyde Park on the north of the river and Quincy on the south. The population increased steadily, and the town had become an affluent and desirable place of residence with proximity to the city.

The Eustis House was designed by William Ralph Emerson and built at 1426 Canton Avenue. The Eustis family had an extensive estate that also had outbuildings designed by owner William Ellery Channing Eustis and the house by the noted architect, who was the "Father of Shingle-style Architecture." Today, it represents one of the last of the great estates of nineteenth-century Milton.

After World War I, many of the remaining farms and the large estates were to be subdivided and developed for residential development. Among these great estates was the Cunningham Estate on Edge Hill Road, which was sold in 1904 to the trustees of the Mary Cunningham Trust to become a park for the benefit of Milton residents, a role it still plays over a century after it was created. The estate was preserved virtually intact, with the mansion later being used as the Milton Convalescent Home and Hospital. Many large estates were systematically developed throughout the town, with house lots being laid out. By the Great Depression, tremendous changes were taking place in Milton. As historian Edward Pierce Hamilton said, by 1929 "the whole character and aspect of our town [changed] in a very great increase in population." In some instances, areas were literally changed beyond recognition, while others had infill development that augmented the area usage with both residential and small commercial development. With the laying out of the Southeast Expressway through Milton in the 1950s, a wide swath was cut through East Milton, virtually dividing the area with a

The Suffolk Resolves House is the headquarters of the Milton Historical Society. Moved in 1950 from Milton Village (the site of the Citizens Bank), it stands at 1370 Canton Avenue, where it was restored by architect-engineer William Morris Hunt II.

suppressed roadbed, ironically, along the path of the Granite Railway, the first railroad in the United States. Granite Avenue was, quite appropriately, to parallel the new highway, and the area of East Milton was to be reconfigured over the next few decades. Other areas of the town, among them Brush Hill, Scots Woods and upper Canton Avenue, remained largely intact, with minor infilling of residences, thereby preserving their semirural character.

One of Milton's greatest claims to fame was that the Suffolk Resolves were signed in Milton in 1774 and were used as a model by the drafters of the Declaration of Independence in 1776. Dr. Joseph Warren led the delegates, who began their resolves that "We acknowledge George III to be our rightful sovereign" but were highly important, outspoken and decisive in their impact. The Daniel Vose House, where the Resolves were accepted and signed by forty delegates before being taken by Paul Revere to the Continental Congress in Philadelphia, still stands and is the headquarters of the Milton Historical Society.

Chapter 1

ARTISTS AND ARCHITECTS

LYDIA SMITH RUSSELL

Lydia Smith Russell was a noteworthy woman even in her own time. An accomplished artist (she had been presented with a medal for drawing from the Emperor Napoleon I), she studied with both Gilbert Stuart and Benjamin West in Boston and with Madame Capan in Paris, where it was her philosophy to "not give away to a belief of the impossibility of uniting, in a girl perfectly educated, accomplishments and duties, which general opinion falsely deems incompatible."

Lydia Smith Russell (1786–1859) was the daughter of Barney and Ann Otis Smith, who lived at Unquety, the former Governor Hutchinson house on Adams Street on Milton Hill. Smith, a wealthy Boston importer of English goods, had purchased the property in 1812 from the estate of Patrick Jeffrey, the former steward of Madame Haley of London, as a home upon his return from Europe. Shortly thereafter, according to Teele's *History of Milton*, he "had not been long on occupation of the place before he began to improve it. He erected the large piazza now standing, and removed the two small, inconvenient wings, which were built with the house and erected the commodious ones now standing, and built a long, circular shed near the north-west corner of the house. These improvements converted a house of ordinary appearance into an imposing structure, for those days."

Lydia Smith Russell (1786–1859) was an accomplished artist who studied art with masters both in Boston and abroad. She lived in Unquity, the Hutchinson Mansion on Milton Hill, and was said to be "an accomplished lady of rare attainments." *Collection of Bayou Bend, Museum of Fine Arts, Houston.*

Here his daughter Lydia lived prior to her marriage, and family and friends of the Smiths were entertained by "the hospitality which always abounded in this mansion, drew a large circle of acquaintances around him, which made it a point of interest, to which many travelers of distinction resorted, where they were magnificently entertained." After almost two decades, the estate was purchased by the Honorable Jonathan Russell (1771–1832) and Lydia Smith Russell at auction in 1829. The Russells had lived abroad for many years, he serving as foreign consul and a minister to several European courts, including as charge d'affairs in Paris, London and Stockholm, and as commissioner to negotiated peace with Great Britain to end the War of 1812. Russell later served as a United States minister to Norway and Sweden from 1814 to 1818. Upon their return to this country, they lived in the mansion with every possible convenience. Russell served as a United States congressman from 1821 to 1823 and died in 1832 after a lingering illness. His widow remained in residence until her own death in 1859.

It was said of Lydia Russell that she was "an accomplished lady of rare attainments [and] did not suffer the character of the house for hospitality and sociability to degenerate…She improved the place by setting out the elms on both sides of the street where the sycamores set out by Governor

Hutchinson, some 100 years before, had died and the house, by making a new and convenient entrance on the south side, which added much to its general appearance and its comfort." The accompanying photograph is of an oval portrait of Lydia Russell, painted by George P.A. Healy (1813–1894) in Boston in 1845; it is today in Bayou Bend, the American Decorative Arts and Painting Collection of the Museum of Fine Arts in Houston, Texas. Painted "a la turque" as a widow, the severity of Lydia's black gown is offset with a lace collar, and she wears a knotted, multicolored silk turban with tassels, often referred to as a mameluke, which was then the height of fashion. Said to be "a worldly, cultured, well-educated artist," she lived in great style and entertained many guests, including friends from Europe such as, in 1849, the Swedish novelist Fredrika Bremer.

Upon her death, the estate was inherited by her children and the portrait was inherited by her daughter Rosalie G. Russell (1822–1887.) The estate was later subdivided, with Hutchinson Street laid out through the property and Russell and North Russell Streets, just west of the house, laid out and named for the family. The house and the portrait were to be inherited by Geraldine Russell Rivers, wife of the author and attorney George R.R. Rivers, Esq.

HAMMATT BILLINGS

Charles Howland Hammatt Billings (1818–1874) was the son of Ebenezer and Mary Davenport Billings who kept the Blue Hill Tavern on Canton Avenue in the early nineteenth century. The tavern had been built in 1681 by Roger Billings, but by the early 1820s, it had become an "elegant tavern, boarding-house, and fruit gardens, kept by Ebenezer Billings , which is one of the most delightful summer retreats in this neighborhood."

Hammatt Billings, as he was to be known in his professional life, was apprenticed about 1830 to the noted wood engraver Abel Bowen, with whom he remained until 1837, when he joined the architectural office of Ammi Burnham Young, who was in the process of designing the Boston Custom House. With his training as an engraver, Mr. Billings was to become a capable designer and trained architect, so when he opened his own architectural office at 460 Washington Street in Boston (now the site of the Registry of Motor Vehicles at the Liberty Tree Building at Washington and Essex Streets) in 1843, he was well rounded in the various aspects of

Mother Goose for Grown Folks was written in 1859 by Adeline Dutton Train Whitney (1824–1906) and illustrated by illustrator-architect Charles Howland Hammatt Billings (1818–1874). The artist created a sketch of a witch opening a blackbird pie as the frontispiece of "A Christmas Reading."

architectural design. Self proclaimed as a "Designer and Architect," Billings often worked with his brother Joseph Billings, who was an engineer. This partnership, a loose one at best, would lead Hammatt Billings to design houses, churches, clubhouses, commercial blocks and libraries throughout New England. His style of architecture, which might be best described as the "classically picturesque," would gain him the commission to design the Boston Museum on Tremont Street in Boston. Designed as an exhibition hall and theatre with monumental Corinthian columns supporting the galleries, the Boston Museum was an early example of the Renaissance Revival in Boston, with a dressed granite façade and arched windows. Mr. Billings later went on to design the campus of Wellesley College between 1869 and his death in 1874. Using a picturesque approach to the overall campus, he laid out serpentine roads leading to impressive buildings that ranged around a lake. A talented and gifted architect, it was said that "he expressed rather than led his generation" in architectural design.

However, his *Monument to the Pilgrim Forefathers*, begun in 1859, was probably his best known design. An eighty-three-foot granite base supported a seventy-foot colossal figure of Faith, who held a book in one hand and pointed toward the Heavens with the other. This monument, of which there is a bronze model on the mantel in the Reading Room of the Milton Public Library, was thought to be the forerunner of Bartholdi's Statue of Liberty, but Faith was not finished until twenty-five years after Billings's death, after having been reduced in size and reworked and altered by other artists. However, his grave in the Milton Cemetery proudly proclaims that he was the "Architect to the Monument to Our Pilgrim Forefathers."

Surprisingly, as an architect Billings had showed great talent, but he never really achieved fame. However, in the designing and illustration of books, which he learned through his apprenticeship with Abel Bowen, he became mildly famous. In 1847, Henry Wadsworth Longfellow called him "the best illustrator of books we have yet had in this country." This was noteworthy praise, as Mr. Billings had illustrated *Mother Goose for Grown Folks*, which was written by Milton authoress Adeline D. Train Whitney. His illustrations were thought to be so good that he was commissioned to create "the original likeness of Tom, Little Eva, Topsy, Legree, and other characters in Harriet Beecher Stowe's *Uncle Tom's Cabin*." His career as an illustrator, like that of his career as an architect, was "breathtakingly varied." He was associated with *Gleason's* as well as *Ballou's Pictorial Drawing Room Companion*, Boston newsweeklies, of which he was one of the numerous illustrators, including Winslow Homer, who made pictorial illustrations.

Though not one who forged ahead in architectural design, Hammatt Billings is one who contributed to the rich fabric of Boston life in the mid-nineteenth century and gave "visible form to the personal, civil, patriotic, and other public sentiments pervasive at the time in Boston and beyond."

DR. WILLIAM RIMMER

William Rimmer was not only a physician but also a noted sculptor, poet, painter and one of the foremost anatomical delineators in the nineteenth century; he and his family lived in East Milton during the mid-nineteenth century. It has been said that Dr. Rimmer was perhaps "the most gifted sculptor in America...an inspired lecturer, who taught several of the next generation's major artists."

Dr. Rimmer (1816–1879) was born in England, the son of Thomas Rimer (later changed to Rimmer). Immigrating to Nova Scotia and thence America in 1818, the family experienced great hardships and were in pecuniary circumstances. The father sincerely believed himself to be the second son of Louis XVI and, therefore, rightful heir to the throne of France. However, he was never able to explain how he was smuggled out of France during the revolution to be raised in South Lancashire, England, with a family who apprenticed him as a boot maker. Settling in South Boston, the Rimmers had five children, and the purported dauphin of France worked as a day laborer and later as a boot maker, the trade to which he had been apprenticed in England.

Though he had given up any hope of being recognized, or believed to be, the lost child of Louis XVI and Marie Antoinette, he often repeated his royal claims to his children, and they are said to have "lived under the psychological, emotional, and social burdens of certain covert expectations that had little possibility of fulfillment." His eldest son, William, actually seems to have believed this tale of royal descent, and "his supposed royal heritage was a central issue, in his life." William helped his family financially as a young man by setting type at newspaper offices, executing lithographs and painting signs, portraits and historical subjects until early middle age.

Though he had an affinity for art, he was unable to earn a living as an artist, so he apprenticed himself to Dr. Abel Washburn Kingman of Brockton for the study of medicine. His later anatomical drawings show not just an artistic depiction of the human body and internal organs but also the fact that he was well aware of the body, its muscles and skeleton and how its internal organs related to the whole. His medical studies, rude at best, made him a typical country doctor who was considered self-educated in the best terminology of the word.

In 1840, Dr. Rimmer married Mary Hazard Corey Peabody, and she provided a stable and supportive environment that allowed his artistic capabilities to evolve. Living in East Milton from 1855 to 1863, first in the Rand House on Adams Street near Pilgrim Road and later in the Stone House on Granite Avenue near the stonecutting sheds of the thriving granite industry, they lived in an ever-active community known as "Railway Village."

The first railroad in the United States was opened in 1826, with cut granite being hauled by horses along tracks laid from the Bunker Hill Quarry in Quincy through the village (now East Milton Square) along Granite Avenue to the Neponset River, where it was loaded onto barges for transport to Charlestown to be used in the erection of the Bunker Hill Monument.

So pervasive and plentiful was granite that Dr. Rimmer actually began in 1858 to carve portrait busts in the hard stone while living in East Milton. However, Dr. Rimmer's art began with oil portraits, landscapes and numerous religious scenes (he painted religious scenes for Saints Peter and Paul in South Boston and St. Mary's in Randolph, as well as the *Massacre of the Innocents* for Dr. Christopher Columbus Holmes of Canton Avenue). His own religious beliefs were broader based, with influences of Transcendentalism and

The Falling Gladiator by William Rimmer (1816–1879) was cast in bronze by Jno. Williams Inc. Bronze Foundry in New York in 1907 from the original plaster model of 1861. Rimmer, who had studied medicine, was considered to be among the finest delineators of the human body in the nineteenth century, and this statue reflects his ability. *Collection of the Metropolitan Museum of Art.*

Spiritualism. In the 1860s, Dr. Rimmer began modeling in plaster, of which his life-size *Falling Gladiator*, commissioned by Stephen Higginson Perkins, was done in East Milton and displayed at his studio as well as in Boston. The plaster model was later cast in bronze in 1907 and was shown in Paris, New York and at the Milton Public Library, after which it was donated by subscription to the Boston Museum of Fine Arts.

Dr. Rimmer began to lecture about art, giving weekly lectures at Fredonia, the Milton Hill home of Mrs. John Murray Forbes, during 1875 and 1877. He began teaching at the School of the Museum of Fine Arts in Boston in 1878, when he displayed his artistic talents, showing paintings of both a compelling interest as well as of ethereal quality with "an element of mystery in every picture." A well-rounded artist, he "considered color, which he believed could by itself express the underlying meaning of an image, to be independent of form...[it] could envelope his image and assist in expressing the sentiment of the subject."

Following both a mental and physical collapse, Dr. Rimmer suspended his art classes and went to stay with his daughter, Adeline A.R. Durham, in South Milford, where he died on August 20, 1879. He was buried on Lilac Path in the Milton Cemetery.

GEORGE HOLLINGSWORTH

George Hollingsworth was the son of Mark and Waitstill Tileston Hollingsworth of Milton. A noted artist in the mid-nineteenth century, he not only painted portraits and bucolic landscapes but also taught painting at the Lowell Institute Drawing School in Boston, training a generation of aspiring artists.

Born in a gambrel-roofed house on what is the north side of Brush Hill Road (on the reservation land opposite the area between Brook Road and Blue Hill Avenue), George Hollingsworth (1813–1882) was the son of Mark Hollingsworth (1777–1855), who was the partner of Edmund Tileston in the paper concern of Tileston & Hollingsworth, established in 1801.

Producing paper in a mill on the Neponset River, the partners were connected not just by business but also by the fact that Mark Hollingsworth married his partner's sister, Waitstill Tileston (1779–1858). In 1815, the Hollingsworths moved to the former Jackson-Boies-McLean House, which

The Hollingsworth Family was painted by George Hollingsworth (1813–1882) in the family home on Brush Hill Road in Milton. Hollingsworth created a fashionable parlor evening, with his family grouped around a pianoforte and his parents seated before the fireplace. *Collection of the Museum of Fine Arts, Boston.*

they purchased in 1824. Their children included George, Anderson, Maria, John Mark, Cornelia, Amor and Lyman Hollingsworth, all of whom would make the house near Mattapan Square a true family home in every sense of the word. The Hollingsworth House was a simple, unpretentious house set near Brush Hill Road with large shade trees on all sides and the Neponset River flowing in the rear.

George Hollingsworth, following his education at Milton Academy, traveled to Italy in 1834, where he began formal training as a painter in Florence. While studying and copying the old masters, he also painted a self-portrait, of which he said he "was a good deal bothered in getting the drawing to look correct when reversed in the mirror." He was more successful when he began planning for a group family portrait, the monumental *Hollingsworth Family of Milton*, which is now at the Boston Museum of Fine Arts. During this period, he sketched and painted and often met with members of the expatriate American colony of artists before returning home. Upon his return, he established a studio in Boston while continuing to live with his parents in Milton.

Mr. Hollingsworth's Boston studio became a welcoming meeting place for artists, and he often socialized as he painted portraits and landscapes.

During his time between Boston and Milton, he became a well-known painter with a theory that art should "draw from the real object or model instead of copying drawings." So adept at art and skillful at teaching was he perceived that he was to become master of the Lowell Institute Drawing School at the Marlboro Chapel in Boston from 1851 until it closed in 1879, ably assisted by William T. Carlton. As early as 1850, the Lowell Institute had a "department of free instruction in the principles and art of drawing and its kindred utilities." Students at the school, both male and female through the suggestion of this skillful master, were admitted as pupils "with the understanding that their good moral character, ability, and skill were accompanied with a taste for drawing and design."

Albert Teele said of him in the *History of Milton* that he had "keen powers and habits of observation, subordinate to the discipline of his profession, imparted a clear intellectual vision and imbued his utterances even in social converse with the charm of originality."

George Hollingsworth was married (in no less than Gilbert Stuart's old studio in Roxbury) to Polly Robbins Eastman of Roxbury in 1859, and they

Standing in front of the Hollingsworth House are Polly Eastman Hollingsworth, George Hollingsworth and their daughter Rose Hollingsworth. *Courtesy of Schuyler Hollingsworth.*

had one child, Rose Hollingsworth (1863–1915.) Upon his father's death in 1855, he came into possession of the family house. Of a typical artist's temperament, Mr. Hollingsworth was described by Mary Hewes Hinckley in an article from 1904 in the *Milton Record* as "a sincere man and a hater of all the shams and insincerities of life. His outspoken manner often concealed his tender heart. He was a man of insight and of a rare wit and humor." He lived with his family a full and contented life on the banks of the Neponset River until his death in 1882.

Following his death, his friends and former students had a bronze relief of George Hollingsworth cast in 1889, which is now at the Boston Museum of Fine Arts. The relief says, "This bronze testifies to the love of his many friends and to the gratitude and esteem of his many pupils." Mr. Hollingsworth had boldly taken advantage of "new opportunities and improved methods to encourage in his pupils works [of art] worthy of intelligent admiration."

Edwin J. Lewis Jr., Architect

Edwin J. Lewis Jr. was a noted architect in Boston a century ago. He was said to be a shy and retiring man, but the fact that he designed over thirty-five churches in the United States and Canada makes him one of the more important architects to have called Milton home. As Mary Fifield King, a friend and resident of one of his houses on Morton Road, said upon his death, "In his profession as an architect he won a high place, and his buildings of great refinement, especially of churches in which he excelled, are found all over New England and beyond."

The son of Edwin J. and Sarah Richards Lewis, Edwin J. Lewis Jr. (1859–1937) was born in Roxbury. His father had emigrated from England and was a successful manufacturer of pickles in Boston, and he built a mansion on Adams Street in Dorchester. Educated at the English High School, Lewis attended the Massachusetts Institute of Technology, which had the first school of architecture in this country, founded in 1867 by William Rotch Ware. Upon his graduation in 1881, Lewis secured a position with the noted Boston architectural firm of Peabody & Stearns. In 1887, he established his own architectural practice, at 9 Park Street on Beacon Hill, and for the next five decades he created a thriving practice "where he continued to go daily during his long professional life." Lewis was to become a post-Medievalist, with his personal interpretation of architecture—be it a residence, meeting hall or place of worship—drawing his inspiration from the Medieval period in England, with half-timbered Tudor Revival houses re-creating, albeit with Victorian comforts and conveniences, the seventeenth-century aspect of architecture brought to this country by the Puritans when they settled Massachusetts Bay Colony in 1630.

Mrs. King said of him that "his work was a good work and his way straight and honorable." However, unlike many architects, he was financially independent and could choose his clients, many of whom were fellow Unitarians, as he was a leading member of the American Unitarian Association. A member of the First Parish in Dorchester on Meeting House Hill, he would design the vestry built in 1912 to the rear of the Cabot, Everett & Chandler–designed church, which was built in 1897 as a high-style Georgian Revival meetinghouse after a fire destroyed the 1816 church. Over fifty years, Lewis was to design impressive, random ashlar quarry-faced stone and wood shingle churches that echoed back to an earlier architectural period and might be considered modified Gothic Revival designs. In Dorchester, he designed Christ Church Unitarian at Dorchester Avenue and Dix Street, and the Peabody, a massive apartment and professional building at Peabody Square commissioned by the Episcopal Diocese of Massachusetts. He also designed the Dedham Historical Society, the Hopedale Community House, All Souls' Church in Braintree, the Roslindale Unitarian (now St. Anna's Orthodox) Church and the First Church of Christ Scientist in Quincy. He designed and built over forty houses that have been identified in Dorchester, as well as five in Milton, among them 77, 86 and 87 Morton Road, as well as two Milton houses for Ridgeway Holbrook, a family friend, at 330 Randolph Avenue and 45 Westside Road.

Lewis was a noted and popular lecturer on history, architectural history and ecclesiastical topics and was an active worker in the city for municipal reform, especially the City Conservation League. He and his two maiden sisters, the Misses Bertha and Marion Lewis, lived in the family mansion in Dorchester until 1923, when they moved to 121 Canton Avenue in Milton; surprisingly, this important architect never lived in a house of his own design. In his fifty years as an independent architect, Lewis maintained memberships in the American Institute of Architects, the Boston Society of Architects (of which he served as secretary), the Boston Athenaeum and the Union Club. Upon moving to Milton, like all good residents should do, he promptly joined the Milton Historical Society; he also served as president of the Dorchester Historical Society from 1917 to 1921. Erudite, educated and well informed, he "lived on the gentler side of life, with books and art and the higher interests of his city, and Boston owes him much."

As Mrs. King said in her tribute to her late friend, "Mr. Lewis would not have asked for tears nor for praise, but for appreciation, perhaps, with esteem and lasting friendships, and these he had."

ROYAL BARRY WILLS, AIA

During the early twentieth century, the interpretation of colonial design was done by many architects, in some cases quite successfully, though the authentic details of the eighteenth century were often adapted for modern-day living. One architect, however, made an important contribution to American architecture and, thanks to the Milton Savings Bank, was able to leave his impressive mark on our town.

Royal Barry Wills (1895–1962) was a noted architect who reintroduced classic eighteenth-century architecture to the public during his long and prodigious career. He once said, "We keep building traditional New England houses because people like them so much. And, if they're kept simple the way they were intended to be, they're almost as modern as Modern." Wills's interpretations of charming classics were to be built throughout the United States and Canada and to accommodate the desire for smaller, more economical yet old-fashioned houses that offered a traditional and long appreciated design.

Following his graduation in 1918 from the Massachusetts Institute of Technology, he began his career with the Turner Construction Company in Boston, but he soon tired of the commercial designs offered by this firm. In 1925, he opened his own architectural office on Beacon Street in Boston, where he designed garrison houses, saltboxes and Cape Cod cottages that began to attract national attention. Following the Depression, his compact yet distinctive designs were taken up with alacrity by a public seeking a sense of economy in new domestic architecture. His designs were so widely appreciated that in 1932 he received a gold medal from President Herbert Hoover for his winning entry in the Better Homes in America Small House Competition. Throughout the 1930–50 period, his firm, known as Royal

The house at 2 Hurlcroft Street was designed by Royal Barry Wills as the Tremont, one of his house designs offered as the "House of the Month" by the Milton Savings Bank. The various designs of single-family houses allowed Wills to offer a variety of Colonial-inspired designs, in both brick and wood clapboard, for post–World War II America. *Author's collection.*

Barry Wills Associates, offered a wide array of designs that could be adapted to suit individual choice and taste. His firm's motto was "No stock plans" and was to result in close to three thousand residential commissions. A prolific author of eight books on architecture, among them *Houses Have Funny Bones* and *Better Houses for Budgeteers*, he had architects in his office whom he "guided and controlled, yet encouraged them to add their individual design talent to the accomplishments of the firm."

Milton has many houses designed by Royal Barry Wills, but it was following World War II that the Milton Savings Bank approached him to design a series of houses that could be used by residents who might build a new house in town and thereby seek a mortgage through the bank. GIs returning from the war were encouraged to build houses for their families, and Wills's "House of the Month" created interest and encouragement. Seen here, the Tremont design was a two-story Colonial with a center chimney that would be built at 2 Hurlcroft Street in Milton, a street laid out in 1942 by Hurley & Driscoll of the Cary Hill Associates, though it is a mirror image of the design seen in the *Milton Record*. The advertisement said that the "charm of this authentic Early American exterior combines narrow white clapboards, louvered shutters of contrasting hue, large capped chimney" and the very necessary one-car garage for modern-day needs. The design, however, was adapted to suit the family and built in red brick, and today it is an impressive residence that perpetuates Royal Barry Wills's vision.

Royal Barry Wills was a respected architect whose vision is kept alive by his family, who continues his architectural office in the Back Bay of Boston. He was awarded a Certificate of Honor in 1949 by the Massachusetts State Association of Architects and in 1954 was elected Fellow of the American Institute of Architects.

Chapter 2
MILTON ARCHITECTURE

MILTON'S FIRST TOWN HALL

Milton has a form of government known as town government, which was established in Dorchester, Massachusetts, in 1633 when "it set the example of that municipal organization which has prevailed throughout New England, and has proved one of the chief sources of its progress."

Dorchester was settled in 1630 by Puritans seeking religious freedom who sailed from England on the ship *Mary and John*. The settlers were people of education and standing, so three years after their arrival in the New World, they were to take the decisive step to form a representative form of governance, as recorded in the *Dorchester Town Records* by James Blake: "This Year [1633] this Plantation began ye practice of Choosing men, that we now call Selectmen or Townsmen. They Chose 12 this year to order ye Affairs of ye Plantation, who were to have their Monthly Meetings, and their orders being confirmed by ye Plantation were full force and binding to ye inhabitants."

James Blake, town clerk of Dorchester and author of the *Annals of the Town of Dorchester*, does not record the names of the first selectmen, but a year later, in 1634, "Mr. Newbury, Mr. Stoughton, Mr. Woolcott, Mr. Duncan, Goodman Phelps, Mr. Hathorne, Mr. Williams, Go. Minot, Go. Gibbes, & Mr. Smith" were elected as representatives of their fellow townsmen.

This organization of a representative form of government was a bold step, and the first order of the selectmen on October 8, 1633, was as follows:

Imprimis it is ordered that, for the general good and well ordering of the affayres of the Plantation their shall be every Mooneday before the Court by eight of the Clocke in the morning, and presently upon the beating of the drum, a general meeting of the inhabitants of the Plantation att the meetinghouse, there to settle (and set down) such orders as may tend to the general good as aforesaid; and every man to be bound thereby without gaynesaying or resistance. It is agreed that there shall be twelve men selected out of the Company that may…meete as aforesaid to determine as aforesaid, yet so as is desired that the most of the Plantation will keepe the meeting constantly and all that are there although none of the twelve shall have a free voice as any of the 12 and that the greate[r] vote both of the 12 and the other shall be of force and efficacy as aforesaid…And shall stand inforce and be obeyed until the next monthly meeting.

As Unquety, a part of Dorchester, was subject to this form of government, it was understandable that it was adopted by the town of Milton when it became an independent township in 1662. For almost 175 years, town meetings were held in Milton at the meetinghouse (now First Parish in Milton, Unitarian). This meetinghouse was not just a place for Sunday worship (morning and afternoon) but also for town meetings, including the monthly selectmen's meetings. A simplistic explanation is that a "town meeting is a single gathering of the voters of the town, called for the purpose of considering those subjects distinctly set forth in the warrant by which the citizens are summoned [and is] a pure democracy, where the citizens as to matters within their jurisdiction, administer the affairs of the town in person."

The selectmen of Milton after 1662 oversaw the collection of taxes, the punishment of miscreants and the appointment of town positions of trust and honor. Within a short period of time, Milton's form of town government had "5 selectmen, 3 Assessors, 1 Bailiff and 2 Constables, 1 Town Clerk, 4 Surveyors of Ways, 1 Sealer of Weights and Measures, 1 Clerk of the Market and 3 Justices for minor cases."

The annual town meeting made appropriations for the ensuing year and included the minister's salary along with colony taxes. This continued, with meetings in March and May, until 1835, when the Unitarian church refused the town of Milton the use of its meetinghouse. For the next two years, meetings were held in the old Academy Building, the Old Stone Church in East Milton or the Railway House, known as the Blue Bell Tavern. However,

The first Milton Town Hall was built in 1837 on the town common between the two churches on Academy Hill, facing Canton Avenue. A simple one-story wood-framed Greek Revival building with a simple pedimented façade, it served the town until 1878. *Courtesy of First Parish in Milton, Unitarian.*

in 1837, the town of Milton built its first town hall. A simple, one-story wood-framed Greek Revival structure with Doric pilasters, the pedimented building was sixty by forty feet and was on the present site of the Lira Bandstand on Milton Common. For the next forty-one years, town government was conducted in this hall, until it was replaced by a larger and more impressive brick town hall designed by Hartwell & Tilden and built in 1878.

Seen in the accompanying photograph, from a detail of a photograph in the collection of the First Parish in Milton, Unitarian, the first Milton Town Hall was a simple affair, with only about 185 voters (out of a total population of 2,241) voting at town meeting in 1850.

THE OLD MILTON TOWN HALL

Following the Civil War, Milton began to experience growing pains, which included an increase in population as well as school-aged children and the inevitable building boom that accompanied this period. All of this translated into the fact that the town hall, built in 1837 on Academy Hill between the First Parish in Milton Unitarian and the First Congregational Church, proved too small for the transaction of the town's business.

In 1878, after approval by town meeting, a new town hall was built on Canton Avenue, on the current site of the Lira Bandstand. Designed by the Boston architectural firm of Hartwell & Tilden, a partnership between Henry W. Hartwell (1833–1919) and George T. Tilden (1845–1919), the new town hall was an impressive Victorian structure of red brick and granite in the Romanesque Revival style. A projecting asymmetrical tower on the façade punctuated the slate roof and had a shorn pyramidal roof cap with cast terra cotta details and ridge caps. Hartwell & Tilden, which was only in existence between 1877 and 1879, was to create an interesting building that provided ample space for town offices and meetings. But the building seemed out of character, at least architecturally, in Milton Centre, with such proximity to the two meetinghouses.

Milton Town Hall was designed by Hartwell & Tilden and built in 1878 on the site of the first town hall. An impressive Victorian structure of red brick and granite in the Romanesque Revival style, it had an asymmetrical tower on the façade. The town hall was replaced, after heated controversy, in 1970 by the present town hall, which was designed by Richard C. Stauffer & Associates. *Author's collection.*

Milton Architecture

Henry W. Hartwell had apprenticed in the architectural office of Charles Howland Hammatt Billings (1818–1874), whose office was at the corner of Washington and Essex Streets in the Liberty Tree Building (now the Registry of Motor Vehicles). Hartwell joined with George T. Tilden of Walnut Street in Milton for two years before he established the architectural firm of Hartwell, Richardson & Driver. These two architects, with a town appropriation of $35,000, worked with the town committee chaired by William Hathaway Forbes with Samuel Gannett, J. Huntington Wolcott, James Murray Robbins, Samuel Babcock, George Vose, Edward L. Pierce, Horace Ware and Reverend Albert Teele to design a building in the prevalent Romanesque style of architecture. Built by the contracting firm of William C. Poland & Sons and with the interior finished by Creesey & Noyes, the town hall was entered through a wide archway entrance with rough hewn granite keystones. A multitude of banked windows had granite lintels, and the foundation was likewise of granite. The interior was finished with quarter-sawn oak woodwork, leaded- and stained-glass windows and heavily trussed ceilings. The hall where town meeting was held, as well as

Milton town meeting in 1955 met in the large auditorium at Milton Town Hall. The interior was finished with quarter-sawn oak woodwork, leaded- and stained-glass windows and heavily trussed ceilings. What was the height of fashion in 1878 had become antiquated and unappreciated just eight decades later.

numerous town-wide events, had a sense of "solid walls, heavy rooftrusses with decorative detailing and pendills," with an enormous gasolier hanging from the center of the ceiling.

Dedicated on February 17, 1879, with Henry S. Russell presiding and Edward L. Pierce presenting the address, the new town hall was as impressive as it was modern, in the Victorian sense of the word. After a ceremony of passing the keys to the selectmen, the Cadet Band entertained the assembled townspeople. The new town hall was described as being "equally well adapted to the town meeting which lies at the foundation of all genuine republican government, and to the social company, which contributes in like measure to the unity and happiness of the people." Throughout the next six decades, the town hall saw great activity and annually hosted town meeting. By the early 1960s, there was increasing agitation for what was referred to as the antiquated Victorian town hall to be replaced with a modern and more spacious town hall. In 1970, the present town hall was built behind the Victorian town hall; designed by Richard C. Stauffer & Associates of Washington, D.C., it has a decidedly 1970s architectural style as one passes it on Canton Avenue. Built by the Quincy contracting firm of Dunphy & Craig, it was opened for town business in 1970, and a year later the old town hall was demolished and the site was graded for a lawn. It would be in 1990, after considerable debate at town meeting, that the bandstand was built through the generosity of Baron Hugo Lira in memory of his wife, Edith Esabella Hamilton Lira.

Though the old town hall was thought "antiquated" and old-fashioned by the 1960s, it was a distinctive building that today might not see demolition because of its architectural importance.

THE LIRA BANDSTAND

The Milton Town Common is located on Canton Avenue between the First Parish in Milton, Unitarian, and the First Congregational Church. Known as Academy Hill, as Milton Academy was originally located on the knoll when it was founded in 1798, today the area is often referred to as the site of the Lira Bandstand, which is prominently located in front of town hall. The Lira Bandstand has been the site of numerous summer concerts. It was the gift in 1990 to the town from Baron Hugo Lira in memory of his wife, Edith Esabella Hamilton Lira, who died in 1980.

Baron Hugo Englebert Lira (1904–1992) was popularly known as "the King of the Totem Pole Ballroom," where he conducted his orchestra between 1942 and 1952. The Totem Pole Ballroom was located in Newton and was widely patronized by people of all ages who reveled in the elegant and surprisingly no-alcohol ballroom. One of the last of the big band leaders at the time of his death, Baron Hugo had formed a thirty-five-piece orchestra in 1936 playing at such important venues as the Riverside in Neponset, Kimball's Starlight Ballroom and Fieldstone-on-the-Atlantic. The band would also play as three- or five-man combos at smaller clubs and often on the Provincetown Boat Cruises and the Moonlight Cruises in Boston Harbor. So well known had Lira and his orchestra become that when he offered the necessary funds to build a bandstand on the town common in memory of his wife, one might have assumed that it would have been accepted with alacrity. However, it was not, and controversy ensued.

The suggested gift of Baron Hugo was widely discussed and greatly debated at town meeting, as the condition of the gift necessitated that it be located on the town common between the two churches. The concern was that Milton Centre, the proposed site of the bandstand, was a historic district designated by the Massachusetts Historical Commission and that the bandstand's design would not fit in with the traditional New England setting. With important town buildings, public art and a lush town common, it was thought that the bandstand would blight the area. After much discussion, town meeting approved of the gift by poll, and it was built in 1990 on the site of the Victorian town hall that had been designed and built in 1878 by Hartwell & Tilden and demolished in 1971.

Dedicated on Veterans Day 1990, town officials and attendees were entertained with a special performance by the Milton High School band after a festive parade to the town common from St. Elizabeth's Church at Keenan Square was held. The bandstand is directly in front of the present Milton Town Hall, which was designed by Richard C. Stauffer & Associates of Washington, D.C., and built in 1970 by the Quincy contracting firm Dunphy & Craig. A decidedly modern building, the town hall is a long, two-story building with a low-pitched roof. The verticality of its windows is correlated with the supporting piers, and it was in marked contrast to the red brick, brownstone and terra cotta town hall demolished. One might wonder why this building was not thought controversial when it was built.

The Lira Bandstand was the gift in 1990 to the Town of Milton from Baron Hugo Engelbert Lira (1904–1992) in memory of his wife, Edith Esabella Hamilton Lira. Known popularly as the "King of the Totem Pole Ballroom," Lira had formed a thirty-five-piece orchestra that played at popular venues throughout New England. *Author's collection.*

Many residents of Milton well remember Baron Hugo for the Miltones, a group of male singers and musicians who told stories through song and entertained in clubs and nursing homes throughout the South Shore. Mr. Lira was an active supporter, both financially and musically, of the Milton High School Band, and Milton Hospital benefited from his volunteer work. His generosity and musical ability were well known, and they were appropriately rewarded in 1984 with a medal from the King of Sweden, which honored Baron Hugo's work on behalf of his fellow Scandinavians in the Boston area. So the next time you pass by the Lira Bandstand or, better yet, enjoy one of the summer concerts, please remember this generous fellow resident of Milton whose career as a musician and bandleader brought joy to our parents' generation and whose generosity in funding the bandstand will bring much joy to generations of Miltonians to come.

The Milton Hill House

The Milton Hill House had been an enduring tradition for over a century and is today represented by a modern, low-rise building on Eliot Street that provides rental apartments and formerly a restaurant on the first floor. Through the last two decades, though the restaurant has often changed hands and names, the welcoming hospitality offered here has often been unsurpassed in town.

The original Milton Hill House was a large Greek Revival mansion with an Ionic colonnade that was built in 1839 on the crest of Morton Hill overlooking the Neponset River. Built by Miss Annette Miller as a school for young ladies, it was built on land owned by the Miller family, who once lived in the Robbins-Cabot-Miller-Morton House, now 78 Morton Road. The Miller family owned almost all of the land along Canton Avenue from Brook Hill Road to High Street and down to Eliot Street; they lived in the large mansion until 1839, when the house was sold to Nathaniel Foster Safford. Mrs. Safford was a daughter of Joseph Morton, for whom Morton Hill was named.

Seen from the Pierce Mill at Dorchester Lower Mills, the Milton Hill House can be seen on the crest of Morton Hill. Built in 1839 as Miss Miller's Female Seminary, it later became the estate of Charles Russell Degan, one-time consul to Turkey, and his wife, Maria Degan. In 1885, the Milton Hill House was opened as a genteel boardinghouse with a loyal clientele.

The school was known as Miss Miller's Female Seminary and was to attract young ladies who both boarded and attended day school, learning such accomplishments as embroidery, sewing, geography, science, literature, French and other such things that would benefit the refined life that these young ladies were expected to lead as adults in the mid-nineteenth century. Though full of promise, the school "was kept for a time, but was soon relinquished," according to Teele's *History of Milton*. Miss Miller lived in town until her death. The Millers sold the lot at the corner of Canton Avenue and High Street to John Durnell, who built the house once occupied by De Wolfe New England; this house was later owned by the noted Milton builder Frederick M. Severence.

Later, the former school and a portion of the land was inherited by Mary K. Whitney, the widow of General Moses Whitney, and upon her death in 1865 it was inherited by her daughter, Maria Degan, the wife of the Honorable Charles Russell Degan. The Degans lived a large part of the year in New York, but would use the house in Milton when they visited Boston. Charles R. Degan once served as consul to Turkey during the mid-nineteenth century, and he and his wife often traveled abroad, bringing back souvenirs from their grand tours.

In 1885, the former Miller-Degan House was opened as a genteel boardinghouse under the direction of resident manager George W. Nickerson. Mrs. Degan, who retained ownership of the property, built 57 Canton Avenue, where she lived until her death in 1893. Upon her death, the Milton Hill House and a large lot of land on Morton Hill was inherited by Theodore Train Whitney and his sister, Caroline Leslie Field, children of Seth and Adeline Train Whitney. George W. Nickerson continued to operate the Milton Hill House under their ownership, and the hospitality of the house became legendary, with many people stopping at the Milton Hill House for extended periods of time in the summer and winter. Often, the attic rooms were rented to young teachers from both Milton Academy and the Glover School on School Street. The house, which served meals and potent libations, was to provide comfortable boarding until 1896, when it was closed for alterations.

When the Milton Hill House reopened, it continued to attract a loyal clientele, some of whom summered on Morton Hill every year. The Greek Revival house had spacious rooms for both boarders and guests and a dining room that even attracted nonresidents for meals. Seen in the accompanying photograph from the early twentieth century, the house was set high on a knoll, offering a pleasant porch with numerous rocking chairs for those who chose to watch as life passed by on Eliot Street. A statement in an advertisement from before World War I extolled the advantages of the Milton Hill House and commented that by "a careful selection of guests… the management has during the past ten years supplied the comforts and attractions of a home of refinement."

Today, though a modern low-rise building has replaced the once elegant Greek Revival mansion, we again revisit and explore its early history.

THE BARTLETT BLOCK

The Bartlett Block, named for owner Jonathan B.L. Bartlett, was a Queen Anne–Tudor Revival red brick building that stood on the triangular lot between the Blue Hills Parkway on the left and Blue Hill Avenue on the right. Built in 1899 adjacent to the owner's home at 75 Blue Hills Parkway, the building had a corner circular tower with a conical roof with stores on the first floor and professional offices above.

In the 1890s, this section of Milton was being developed but still had large estates, among them Briarfield, the five-acre Tileston Estate between Eliot Street and Brook Road, the two-acre Clary Estate near Eliot Street, the five-acre Eliza George Estate at the corner of Brook Road and the Blue Hills Parkway and the six-acre former Cornell-Austin Estate on Blue Hills Parkway that, in 1889, had become the Leopold Morse Home for Aged and Infirmed Hebrews and Orphans. The redesigning of Mattapan Street (now known as the Blue Hills Parkway), which extended from the Neponset River to Canton Avenue, in the 1890s by the Olmsted Associates of Brookline created a dual roadway on either side of a green strip that had trees planted to create an alley from Mattapan to Unquity Road, the entrance to the Blue Hills Reservation.

The Bartlett Block was built as a commercial building facing Mattapan Square, with a clock in the gable facing the intersection. With the Blue Hill Street Railway leaving Mattapan Station and passing the block as it proceeded up Blue Hill Avenue, this Queen Anne–Tudor Revival building made an important impression on those who saw it. The Blue Hill "horseless carriages" can be seen on either side of the photograph. Planted with a

The Bartlett Block was at the junction of the Blue Hills Parkway, on the left, and Blue Hill Avenue. Named for Jonathan B.L. Bartlett, the Queen Anne–Tudor Revival red brick commercial building was built in 1899, with a corner circular tower with a conical roof and a clock in its gable. *Author's collection.*

double alley of trees, the parkway was an impressive green strip that connected the more built up area of town near Mattapan and the entrance to the bucolic and rural Blue Hills Reservation at Unquity Road. On the far right, which is not depicted in the photograph, is one of only three "three deckers" in Milton, built in 1905 at the triangular junction of Blue Hill Avenue and Brush Hill Road. Though numerous three deckers were eventually built in Dorchester and Mattapan, Milton took decisive action by the banning of multiple-family dwellings by enacting the Tenement Act. In the December 21, 1912 edition of the *Milton Record*, it was noted with concern that "some action in this matter was emphasized by the statement of the [Milton] Inspector of Buildings that a six-tenement three decker is to be erected in East Milton." With this, it was emphasized in 1912 that the legislature, through the Tenement House Act for Towns, prohibited "three family tenements unless they are of fireproof construction." With such stringent regulations, and majority acceptance by town meeting, no further three deckers could be built, which might have radically changed the character of the area to a great extent. However, the Bartlett Block was demolished when the traffic flow at Mattapan Square was redesigned.

Chapter 3

TOWN SERVICES AND DEVELOPMENT

MILTON'S CIVIL WAR MONUMENT

Milton's Civil War Monument is between the First Parish Unitarian-Universalist and the Lira Bandstand, facing Canton Avenue. A cast bronze eagle alights from a boulder, commemorating those men from Milton who served in the Civil War between 1861 and 1865.

In 1934, remarkably sixty-nine years after the end of the Civil War, the town of Milton moderator appointed a committee, composed of Jesse B. Baxter, Charles Bradlee, Sarah E. Holmes, Dora A. McCue and Albert L. Schindler, to erect a "Memorial to the Union Veterans of the Civil War." The committee decided upon a spread-winged eagle alighting from a boulder, the design of which was approved by the Milton Art Commission. The boulder was found in the Blue Hill Reservation and given to the town by the Metropolitan District Commission; the eagle was then cast by T.E. McGann & Sons of Boston, a noted bronze foundry, by "a man in their employ"; however, the name of the sculptor was not given. This eagle was an obviously popular choice, for McGann & Sons provided identical bronze casts of the eagle to the towns of Lincoln and Hillsboro, New Hampshire. The committee asked Reverend Markham W. Stackpole, chaplain of Milton Academy, to compose the inscription, which simply states, "In grateful memory of our citizens who served in the Civil War 1861–1865." The monument was appropriately dedicated on October 7, 1934, with the honored presence of James Byrnes, the sole surviving Civil War veteran.

A parade of veterans left the American Legion headquarters on Brook Road and, escorted by the American Legion Band Drum Corps, marched along Thacher and Lincoln Streets, Brook Road and Canton Avenue before it reached the monument. The monument was then dedicated by Commander Byrnes using the Grand Army Dedication Ritual, ably assisted by the Sons of Union Veterans. The grandchildren of Commander Byrnes unveiled the bronze tablet, and a dedicatory oration was read by Reverend Stackpole.

Today, this monument is shaded by lush shrubbery, and the bronze eagle can be seen with his wings spread wide and his talons grasping the boulder. The year 2001 marked the 140th anniversary of the beginning of the Civil War, when some of our fellow townsmen left Milton to defend the Union of the United States and gave the ultimate sacrifice for their country. These men are: George Baxter, George F. Bent, Lieutenant Josiah Bent Jr., Amos H. Bronsdon, William A. Buckley, George W. Burditt, N.

The Milton Civil War Monument commemorates those men from Milton who served in the Civil War between 1861 and 1865. The bronze eagle was cast by T.E. McGann & Sons of Boston and surmounts a large boulder that was dedicated in 1934. *Author's collection.*

Stanley Everett, Lieutenant Josiah H.V. Fidd, Allen C. Griswold, George W. Hall Jr., Elijah M. Hunt, Isaiah Hunt, Samuel Hunt Jr., Lieutenant Albert Jackson, George Long, Martin Lyons, Albert T.B. Martin, Captain Joseph W. Morton, Nathaniel T. Myers, Joseph A. Parsons, Lieutenant Stephen G. Perkins, Captain J. Sewall Reed, W.O.V. Rockwood, John Scaff, Major General Edwin Vose Sumner, Lieutenant George W. Thacher, Charles H. Thayer, George Ellis Vose, T. David Vose and Lieutenant Huntington Frothingham Wolcott.

MILTON POLICE

The present Milton Police Headquarters is a large Colonial-style building at 40 Highland Street, the corner of Highland Street and Canton Avenue. It was built in 1973 on a portion of the former Touzalin-Pierce Estate that had been sold to the town in 1948 by Vassar Pierce for the Milton Hospital. In 2010, the Milton Police Department, now headed by Chief of Police Richard Wells, celebrated the 120th anniversary of its founding, and it is an

Members of the Milton Police Department pose in front of the police station in 1905. The lockup was built in 1884 by J.H. Burt and Company at the town landing on Wharf Street in Milton Village. Today, the Milton Yacht Club uses the building as its headquarters.

important town service that has earned the respect and perpetual thanks of all who call Milton home.

The first organized police force in Milton was established in 1890; previously, a town constable and three night watchmen served the town until 1874, when Samuel O. Hebard (1843–1916) was appointed the first full-time policeman. With a population of 4,728 in 1890, Milton was a relatively quiet beat; however, in 1884 the town had commissioned J.H. Burt & Company of Mattapan, a building firm composed of brothers John H. Burt and George L. Burt, to build a red brick lockup with five retaining cells on Wharf Street in Milton Village. This police station and lockup was a simple red brick and granite lintel building with an end gable roof with a superintendent's office where Edwin A. Houghton took calls from the town's thirteen street alarm call boxes and welcomed the occasional vagrant to the lockup. The building, which is now used as the headquarters of the Milton Yacht Club, is unassuming and remained as such for its first two decades until 1906, when the police department moved to Central Avenue.

In 1890, Maurice Pierce, a former policeman, became the first chief of police. His force initially consisted of three patrolmen during the day (one patrolman each at Mattapan, East Milton and Milton) and fourteen patrolmen at night. It seems obvious that crime in Milton manifested itself at night, for with fourteen patrolmen on night duty, one can well imagine what nefarious activities took place after the workday. As the town grew, it was decided in 1906 by town meeting to purchase the former Milton Light & Power Company building on Central Avenue. This large brick and stucco building, built in 1890 by local resident Edwin T. Ruggles, was a coal-fired steam generator station that provided power for hundreds of Milton residences, as well as commercial property and streetlights. The power station was purchased in 1903 by the Edison Electric Illumination Company when the Milton Light & Power was merged with the larger utility company. The building, which stood on Central Avenue, now the site of a former town parking lot at Edward T. O'Neill Square, was purchased by the Town of Milton and, offering much more space than the lockup on Wharf Street, was promptly renovated for its new and expanded services. By 1906, Milton's population had increased to 7,203 and was a widely settled town. A horse-drawn patrol wagon, which often doubled as an ambulance, traveled through the town and kept it free from crime. Surprisingly, it was the "horseless carriage" that posed many of

Chief of Police Maurice Pierce sits in his Stanley Steamer in front of the flag- and bunting-bedecked Central Avenue Police Station in 1912. Officer Fallon, dapperly dressed, served as his chauffeur. The police headquarters had been built in 1890 as the Milton Light and Power Company, designed by Edwin T. Ruggles, and served as police headquarters from 1906 to 1973.

the problems at the beginning of the twentieth century. Automobiles had begun to be used in greater numbers, but their noise often scared horses and scattered both people and animals as they traveled through the town. It is said that the first arrest for automobile speeding in Milton was in 1900, but in each subsequent year the *Milton Record* gives speeding statistics that seem unbelievable. So great had the number of speeding arrests become that a motorcycle was purchased in 1907 by the town so that the police could deal with recalcitrant motorists, ninety-three of whom were arrested in that year alone.

Mr. Pierce, as the first chief of police, instilled a sense of professionalism in his department that has been maintained to this day. It was once said that "all in all the law enforcement department of Milton represented by a corps of young and alert men keeps the town remarkably free from crime." Succeeding Pierce as chief of police was James R. Travers, followed by Timothy McDermott, John B. Shields, John E. Whearty, Dennis J. Doyle, Gerard R. Mattaliano, Richard G. Wells, Kevin J. Mearn and present chief of police Richard G. Wells Jr. and Charles F. Paris, deputy chief. With the present number of policemen and policewomen, in addition to modern police cars, we again remember the early years of the police department a century ago when a horse-drawn patrol wagon represented the sole police response unit in town.

THE MILTON RED CROSS

The Red Cross is an international society for the relief of suffering in time of war or disaster. The Red Cross began, unofficially, with the many nurses who served during the Civil War, headed by Clara Barton, who "ministered relief to those in distress throughout the world." During World War II, the Red Cross was an important part of Milton's wartime efforts with a determined and compassionate group of civilian volunteers who acted as first aid workers, street and dark-out wardens and motor corps drivers.

The committee that formed the Metropolitan Chapter of the American Red Cross was headed by Aimee Alssop, who induced a group of Milton residents to meet at the Milton Public Library to provide assistance to "the troops [which] were summoned in June of 1916" for the Allies to fight the Axis countries.

The Motor Corps of the Milton Chapter, American Red Cross, flank a Red Cross wagon in 1949. *From left*: Mrs. Robert S. Wallace, Miss Katherine S. Gould, Mrs. Robert Cody, Mrs. Stanley Harwood, Miss S. Frances Marden, Mrs. Newlin B. Wildes, Chairman Mrs. Clarence H. Jones Jr., Mrs. Nathaniel Cutler and Mrs. Nathaniel C. Lord. *Author's collection.*

The Milton chapter was chaired by W. Rodman Peabody, a noted attorney, and the secretary-treasurer was Anne Whitney; it was said after its official formation in May 1916 that the Milton Red Cross committee "was practically the only one in the State which was organized with subcommittees and efficiently working." Among the early volunteers were Mrs. James Lawrence, Mrs. John Monroe, Mrs. M. Vassar Pierce, Mrs. Philip Y. De Normandie, Mrs. Robert Saltonstall, Mrs. Samuel Johnson, Mrs. Philip Dalton and Mrs. W.W. Churchill. Each of these war relief volunteers oversaw committees that prepared surgical dressings, preparations for first aid and home nursing, sewing, fundraising and publicity. So successful were these women that in 1918, through weekly meetings at the Milton Club on Central Avenue, they raised just over $122,000, which was "471 percent of the quote assigned" to Milton. With this stupendous effort, a Red Cross Honor Flag was raised at the Red Cross Headquarters (the former Thacher School) on Walnut Street, along with the even greater honor of "naming a ship of the emergency fleet" of the United States.

During this time, a local blood bank was established and effectively organized by Mrs. Edward Wallace; this drive would prove a major program that secured whole blood for not just the Red Cross but also Milton Hospital. Though the Milton Red Cross came to an official end following World War II, an office was maintained at town hall until it was later moved to Milton Hospital. The Milton Red Cross would continue efforts on behalf of the growing needs in the community with a "willingness to work for the benefit of their fellow townsman and to enlist the help of others when aid was needed under the banner of the Red Cross which flies over all lands, and under all conditions where help of any kind is needed."

Today, decades after our fellow townsmen were induced by Aimee Alssop to form a Milton chapter of the Red Cross, we fully realize how important its efforts have been in both wartime as well as peacetime by answering as many requests for assistance as it was capable.

THE CHILDREN'S TILE WALL

You may not have noticed it as you passed it, but the Milton Public Library has a wall of 322 colorful tiles that were painted by Milton schoolchildren at the instigation of the Milton Rotary to specifically adorn the wall of the new addition to the Central Library. Designed by Shepley, Bulfinch, Richardson

Pointing to her "square of fame" is young library patron Mary Henderson, along with Elaine McDermott, Joseph Kelley and teacher Harriet Hamlin; they were among the 1,700 Milton students who submitted entries for the children's tile wall, sponsored by the Milton Rotary Club. The work was implemented by Julian B. Alexander and Harriet Dora Hamlin, who "gave untiring and inspired support in organizing the efforts of the children in creating the tile transfers." *Courtesy of the Milton Public Library.*

& Abbott, the successor architectural firm to Shepley, Rutan & Coolidge, who had designed the central library in 1902, the 1957 library addition was a decidedly modern wing with large plate-glass windows, doors and a more open design than the original library.

Seen in the accompanying photograph is Diane Pawley, the then children's librarian, with three of the young artists whose sketches "were transferred to the tile with white graphite paper and each 'artist' applied his own underglaze" to the tiles for the eight- by nine-foot wall with illustrations of popular books or stories. Pointing to her "square of fame" is young library patron Mary Henderson, along with Elaine McDermott and Joseph Kelley, who were among the 1,700 Milton students who submitted entries. The Milton Rotary, Dr. John F. Gallagher as president, fully supported this project, which was implemented by Julian B. Alexander and Harriet Dora Hamlin, art teachers who "gave untiring and inspired support in organizing the efforts of the children in creating the tile transfers." What amazes me most about this photograph isn't that it shows the tile wall as a combined effort of many people that was successfully carried to completion but how well dressed the children are! I suppose that 1957 was a far different time when compared to today, but I marvel at how neatly pressed the girls' dresses are and how the boy's pocket handkerchief stands out against his blazer.

The Milton Rotary approached the Milton Public Schools with the concept of a tile wall, but the idea was taken up with alacrity by the Art Department, and primary and middle school students were soon painting an unglazed square tile with their own unique design, which was then glazed and fired. The Milton Rotary then had a tile with its logo placed in the center of the wall, stating, "Sponsored by the Milton Rotary Club 1958," and the individual tiles were arranged around it. One can imagine the excitement of the young artists as they searched for their tile and then proudly pointed it out to their parents.

THE RUSSELL READING ROOM

At the turn of the century, the Milton Public Library opened a reading room in the Scotts Woods section of Milton for residents of Milton who lived too far to walk to the library at Milton Village. In 1898, according to Nathaniel Kidder's *First Sixty Years of the Milton Public Library*, Mrs. Henry Sturgis Russell offered to the library trustees the use of a room in a building on her estate, which was located at the junction of Randolph Avenue and Hillside Street. After considerable debate, the trustees decided to open a "branch of the library" for a specific period of time "if incurring no expense to the Town" and, if it proved successful, to operate it as a permanent branch library. In 1899, the library trustees "voted to take over full charge of the Russell reading room [at Scotts Woods] as the six months' trial had demonstrated its value." It obviously had demonstrated its value, as the circulation in one year (1899 to 1900) increased from 19,168 books to 31,367 books borrowed.

The Russell Reading Room, which was named for Mary Hathaway Forbes Russell (1844–1916)—the wife of Colonel Henry S. Russell, whose Milton estate was known as the Home Farm—was a fairly large wood shingle building that had previously been used for a variety of purposes. Wired for electricity in 1901, the circulation of books there was never as great as at the main library, but it proved that a branch library and reading room was of decided interest to town residents and was obviously used. In many ways,

The Russell Reading Room of the Milton Public Library was on a corner of the Russell Estate at Randolph Avenue and Hillside Street. In 1898, Mary Hathaway Forbes Russell (1844–1916) offered the use of a room in a building on her estate, and the branch was later moved to a large wood shingle building at the corner of Randolph Avenue and Hillside Street. *Courtesy of the Milton Public Library.*

this reading room proved to be the catalyst for the opening of the Kidder Branch near Mattapan and the East Milton Branch by the library trustees. Today, the site of the Russell Reading Room has been developed for large houses on Heather Drive and Mark Lane.

THE OLD KIDDER BRANCH LIBRARY

Some seem to think that with the move of the Tuell-Smith House at 488 Canton Avenue to allow for the expansion of the public library, this was the first time such a thing was attempted in town, but in 1929, another house was moved to make way for the new Kidder Branch of the Milton Public Library. The former Kidder Branch Library was jacked up and placed on wood cribbing prior to its removal from Blue Hills Parkway to its new location on Chilton Park.

The former library was a carpenter-built, Victorian, one-family house with gables on all four sides that had been built by William H. Crosby, a well-known builder at the turn of the century. Mr. Crosby had developed and

Town Services and Development

The Kidder Branch of the Milton Public Library was named for Henry Thayer Kidder, chairman of the library trustees. The building had formerly been used by the Kidder Community Center, founded in 1911 as a "sort of community house, with accommodations for a boys' club and for a reading room." In 1928, the library was moved to 24 Chilton Park, where it was remodeled as a house, and a new branch library was designed by Eliot T. Putnam. *Courtesy of Linda Pirie.*

built entire streets in the area near Mattapan, such as Churchill and Tucker Streets and Concord and Dyer Avenues. This two-story, wood-framed house at 101 Blue Hills Parkway was later purchased in 1911 with three adjoining lots by Nathaniel Thayer Kidder and others "to organize experimentally a sort of community house, with accommodations for the boys' club (recently organized by Roger Ernst) and for a reading room."

Mr. Ernst was a graduate from Harvard and worked with the boys at Kidder House following his graduation. The Kidder Community Center—which had been incorporated in 1910 by Nathaniel T. Kidder, M. Vassar Pierce, Nathaniel Stone, Harry K. White and Roger Walcott—served a very necessary purpose as a safe as well as fun place for youth to go after school and on Saturdays. In the same vein as the settlement houses of a generation earlier, such as Dorchester House, Norfolk House in Roxbury and the West End House and the Elizabeth Peabody House in Boston's West End, the center was to provide guidance and experience to boys and young men while

Nathaniel Thayer Kidder (1860–1938) was a noted philanthropist and Milton's first tree warden. Son of Henry P. Kidder, a co-founder of Kidder, Peabody & Company, he was graduated from Harvard College and later attended the Bussey Institute. He served as president of the trustees of the Milton Public Library, the Museum of Fine Arts and the Massachusetts General Hospital and was largely responsible for providing the funds to build the Milton Public Library, designed by Shepley, Rutan and Coolidge and built in 1904. *Author's collection.*

offering a branch library to all. By the fall of 1911, the small library of books and periodicals belonging to the Milton Public Library and housed in the Bartlett Building in Mattapan was moved to the Kidder House, which was under the auspices of the Kidder House Association, and the branch library was opened for all of the residents of this area of Milton. In addition to serving as a small branch library, the house and a barn in the rear of the property were used for boys' club, with a gymnasium and clubrooms. Though cramped for space, the annual circulation of books, which were housed on the first floor, had reached 27,335 by 1925. The Kidder House Association offered the house and land to the town in 1928, and it was accepted at town meeting. Shortly thereafter, the Kidder House was moved along the parkway to 24 Chilton Park, where alterations were made to return the house to single-family usage. It was sold by the town to Mr. and Mrs. Clyde L. Whittier to benefit the construction of a new branch library.

Eliot T. Putnam (1880–1946) was a partner with Joseph Chandler in the Boston architectural firm of Putnam and Chandler and was engaged as architect to design both the new Mattapan and East Milton Branch libraries. The Mattapan Branch was officially named the Kidder Branch in honor of Nathaniel Thayer Kidder (1860–1938).

Chapter 4
BUSINESSES AND BUSINESSPEOPLE

ISAAC SANDERSON'S PAPER MILL

Isaac Sanderson was one of a group of prominent paper manufacturers once located along the Neponset River. As early as 1728, a group of investors opened a paper mill that reputedly produced the first paper in New England, and they were given the sole right to manufacture paper for a term of ten years. James Boies and Hugh McLean, two men from Northern Ireland, later operated a paper mill at what is now Mattapan Square, and the Sumner Mill was upriver at what eventually became Hyde Park. The Tileston and Hollingsworth Paper Company was to become one of the leading manufacturers of paper in the area in the nineteenth century, and among them was Isaac Sanderson.

Isaac Sanderson was born in Watertown, Massachusetts, and married Betsey Gill (1777–1858). Their daughter, Elizabeth, married Moses Whitney Jr. (1802–1844) of Adams Street in Milton Village. The Sandersons lived in a large house in Milton Village on a low plain to the left as one crossed the river heading south (now the site of the Extra Space Storage Company). Adjacent to his home was a three-story wood-framed paper mill (which happens to be for sale at the present time) that had been built in 1728 for Jeremiah Smith, who manufactured paper here. In this mill, beginning in 1801 when he moved to Milton Village, Sanderson made paper, like others, from rags collected throughout the area. However, Sanderson was an

The Sanderson Mill at Milton Village was on the south bank of the Neponset River. Here Isaac Sanderson produced paper, as well as beach grass paper that won him awards from the Massachusetts Charitable Mechanics Association. *Author's collection.*

enterprising paper manufacturer, and in 1803, he was to manufacture for the Boston Custom House, then located on Custom House Street in Boston, the first folio-post and quarto letter paper made in New England. In 1817, Sanderson installed the first iron tub wheels in New England in his paper mill in Milton Village, a marked improvement from the old wood tub wheels.

Not only was Sanderson's rag paper a resounding success, but beginning in the 1830s, he also began to experiment in the manufacture of paper from beach grass, which grew in abundance along the marshes located east of the town landing. The long, flat leaves of beach grass closely resemble papyrus and, when dried, are able to be made into a form of parchment that was unusual but highly successful and useful. This experimentation led to Sanderson's recognition from the American Institute of New York, which presented him a silver medal "for paper made from beach grass" in 1838; the Mechanics Institute of New York "for specimens of beach grass writing paper" in 1838; and the Massachusetts Charitable Mechanics Association "for specimens of beach grass paper" in the exhibition of 1839. Sanderson was always dapperly dressed in a jabot and waistcoat, proudly wearing his silver medals on a chain. The medals are today preserved in the Milton Historical Society's collection.

Following Sanderson's death, Dr. Jonathan Ware (1797–1877) purchased the Sanderson House and mill and erected a new mill with two reaction wheels, which allowed the waters of the Neponset River, via guide vanes, to go into the wheel and downward axially, escaping at the bottom. Dr. Ware's Chocolate Company began in 1843 and for the next few decades was a stiff competitor of both the Baker Chocolate Company as well as the Webb & Twombley Chocolate Company in the village until 1881, when the concern was purchased by Henry L. Pierce and merged with Baker Chocolate Company. In 1892, the old Sanderson-Ware House was demolished, and the circular storage warehouse, probably designed by Winslow & Wetherall, was built by Henry L. Pierce. Surprisingly, the old wood paper mill survives to this day and is probably the oldest structure in Milton Village.

JAZANIAH FORD

The accompanying playing card was printed in Milton in 1825 by Jazaniah Ford, a playing card manufacturer who lived on the east side of Highland Street at the crest of the hill near Spafford Road. Mr. Ford probably used cardstock paper manufactured at Mattapan by the Tileston & Hollingsworth Paper Mill to make his cards. A skilled manufacturer of "the profane with the instruments of perdition," he had learned his trade from Thomas Crehore (1769–1846), with whom he was once in partnership. Crehore manufactured playing cards on River Street in Dorchester Lower Mills as early as 1800 and is thought to have been among the first playing card manufacturers in this country.

Mr. Crehore—whose brother, Benjamin Crehore, was a pianoforte and bass viol manufacturer in Milton Village—and Mr. Ford produced fine quality playing cards that were protected from imports as early as 1812 by a hefty duty and later a large rate after 1846. Mr. Ford (1757–1832) married Abigail Sumner (1760–1835), the daughter of Seth and Lydia Babcock Sumner of Milton. After their marriage, they lived in the house of her brother, Dr. Enos Sumner (who practiced in town from 1770 to 1796), which had been built in 1771. On a portion of this property, Mr. Ford opened his locally famous playing card factory. This playing card has an image of the Marquis de Lafayette (1757–1836), who was a hero of the American Revolution and was making his triumphal tour of the United States in honor of the fiftieth anniversary of the Revolution. On his return to Boston, he was entertained at the Milton Hill mansion of Dr. Amos Holbrook, a veteran himself of the Revolution, so he was as well known locally as he was nationally. The card has Lafayette's image in a banded reed cartouche

Jazaniah Ford produced playing cards on Highland Street in Milton. This card, a spade, depicted the Marquis de Lafayette in a cartouche with an eagle surmounting it with a fluttering ribbon stating "American Manufacture." Lafayette toured the United States in 1825 on the fiftieth anniversary of the American Revolution.

with an American eagle surmounting it with a fluttering ribbon extolling its "American Manufacture." At the base is a black spade with a cannon and an American flag crossed with laurel and oak leaves on either side. These playing cards, printed "JAZh. FORD," were popular not just as playing cards but also as mementos of Lafayette's visit and were as collectible in 1825 as they are today.

The playing card factory on Highland Street was destroyed by fire in 1861, and the old Sumner-Ford-McQuirk House was eventually demolished after a fire by 1880. Today, the only memorial to this early playing card manufacturer is his name on the black granite monument set on the Sumner Family Tomb in the Olde Burying Grounds in Milton Cemetery.

THE GRANITE RAILWAY COMPANY

The Granite Railway was the first railroad built in America. Built to connect the granite quarries in Quincy to the Neponset River, the three-and-a-half-mile route extended along Willard Street in Quincy and along Granite Avenue in Milton, terminating at a wharf where the granite was unloaded from the railway cars by a crane and placed on sloops to be shipped to Charlestown. The granite industry commenced in 1826 to provide a supply of granite for the Bunker Hill Monument in Charlestown. The cornerstone of the monument's soaring obelisk was laid in 1825 by the Marquis de Lafayette when he toured the United States on the fiftieth anniversary of the Revolution. Gridley Bryant, a noted engineer, created the means for the Granite Railway Company, which was obtained in March 1826, with Colonel Thomas H. Perkins serving as president and the incorporators being Perkins, William Sullivan, Amos Lawrence, David Moody, Gridley Bryant and Solomon Willard. The first horse-drawn cars loaded with granite from the Bunker Hill Quarry in Quincy began service on October 7, 1826, and began an operation that would continue for the next four decades. The route from Quincy to the Neponset River had a slight decline, so the horses used to pull the cars were not overexerted in their job. Seen in the accompanying photograph, a team of horses pulling granite-filled cars stops at the junction of Adams Street and Granite Avenue about 1860; the houses in the distance were on Adams Street between Granite Avenue and Franklin Street in the area then known as Railway Village. With empty cars, the horses did not have a burden to pull the cars back to Quincy.

The railway designed by Gridley Bryant to transport granite from the Bunker Hill Quarry to the Neponset River is considered the first railway in the United States. Horses, stopped at the intersection of Adams Street and Granite Avenue, pulled gondola cars filled with quarried granite that would be dressed in Railway Village (East Milton) before being sent to Charlestown to be used in the building of the Bunker Hill Monument.

The route had a gauge of five feet with stone sleepers placed at eight-foot intervals. Upon the sleepers were placed wooden rails six inches wide and twelve inches high. Three-inch iron plates were fastened to these rails with spikes; however, they were replaced after a few years with stone rails for greater durability and longevity. The quality of the construction, along with the natural decline in topography to the Neponset River, made for little maintenance, and it continued with little infusion of funds for many years. The Granite Railway, which spurred the residential development of Railway Village (present-day East Milton), attracted numerous visitors who came to see the operation. After observing the operation, they often visited the Blue Bell Tavern, a granite building on Adams Street and the present site of the post office. Known as the Railway House, Railway Hotel and the Blue Bell Tavern, the inn provided hot meals and potent libations for both the visitors and the workmen of the granite industry. During the first two decades, the Blue Bell Tavern (called as such for the blue bell that was rung by the tavern keeper when meals were ready) was not the only building to be constructed of granite in Milton. Luther

The Howe House was built at the corner of Reedsdale Road and Randolph Avenue completely of triangular pieces of granite from the Bunker Hill Quarry in Quincy. There were several buildings in Milton constructed of granite, with this house being the only surviving structure. Today, the house is part of St. Elizabeth Church. *Author's collection.*

Felt's blacksmith shop was built at the comer of Adams and Squantum Streets, and the Howe House was built at the corner of Reedsdale Road and Randolph Avenue. These buildings of Quincy granite survive as testimony to its durability as both a building material as well as its use in stone walls, piers and markers throughout town. Begun for the Bunker Hill Monument, the granite quarries in Quincy were also to be used for the building material of the Boston Custom House (1847, Ammi Burnham Young), the Tremont House Hotel (1829, Isaiah Rogers) and Boston's city hall (1863, Gridley J. Fox Bryant).

Though before 1800 few buildings were built of granite (the only two I know of were the Hancock House (1737) on Beacon Hill and King's Chapel in Boston), it became a building material of choice of architects and builders by 1830.

BAKER CHOCOLATE PROFIT-SHARING PLAN

Not only is the Baker Chocolate Company in the Lower Mills–Milton Village the oldest manufacturer of chocolate in the United States (founded in 1765 and established in 1780), but it is also one of the first large companies in this country to establish and annually contribute to a profit-sharing plan established for the benefit of its employees.

Profit-sharing plans, as well as 401K plans, are one of the many inducements used to retain key employees who make substantial contributions to the operation of a company. A plan that gives employees a share of the profits of the company is a great way to instill a sense of ownership of the company in employees and thereby extract high expectations and hopefully lengthy service from them. However, it was in 1904 that the Forbes Syndicate—which had purchased the profitable

This broadside of Walter Baker & Company depicted the Pierce Mill (designed by Nathaniel J. Bradlee and built in 1872) on the Dorchester side of the Neponset River. Established in 1780 by Dr. James Baker, the chocolate company was one of the largest employers on the South Shore of Massachusetts and remained until 1965, when it moved to Dover, Delaware. *Courtesy of Boston Athenaeum.*

chocolate company in 1897 for $4.75 million from the estate of Henry L. Pierce—gave a week's salary to four hundred employees of the chocolate mills with one year or more of service as extra compensation.

In 1905, the Baker Chocolate Company was quoted by the *Boston Transcript*, a leading newspaper of the day, in a letter to employees as saying that the "directors of Walter Baker & Co. Limited, are pleased to be able to enclose with your pay this week a check the amount of which is based on the number of days' service in employ of the company during the last year. It is recognized by the company that your ***personal efforts and interest*** [author's emphasis] will insure the continued high quality of our product, thus making our business success permanent." The article went on to say that "the company showed its interest in the welfare of its people last week by enclosing in the envelope of each employee a check for an amount of money equal to ten percent of his or her earnings during 1904."

Well, a 10 percent profit-sharing check is a substantial one, but it was more importantly a manifestation that the company management sincerely realized that the employees were an important part of the success of the Baker Chocolate Company. Shortly thereafter, further incentives were instituted: in 1909, management reduced the fifty-eight-hour workweek to fifty-six hours; in 1916, an eight-hour workday was instituted with time and a half for extra hours; in 1922, cooperative group life insurance plans were offered to employees; in 1934, a cooperative retirement plan for employees was established; in 1936, a vacation with pay plan was established; and in 1937, a sickness benefit plan was put in place.

All in all, a job at the Baker Chocolate Company was not just something that was obviously appreciated and rewarded by the management but also a delicious one.

THE MILTON BOOKMOBILE

In the accompanying photograph, Ernest Leavitt and Frank Farrington stand with the horse-drawn delivery wagon of the Milton Public Library behind the library about 1910 awaiting books that would be distributed from house to house in Milton. It is said in the centennial history of the library that it is thought that "this mobile book delivery was one of the first in the United States."

In 1901, the Milton Public Library was located in the Associates Building, which was designed by Rotch and Tilden and built on Adams Street in Milton Village in 1882. A large part of Milton was inaccessible to Milton Village due to the distance involved, so the library trustees voted to establish a horse-drawn "bookmobile" to provide library books to the public in a decidedly novel approach. In the records of the Milton Public Library, it was recorded that this "is an experiment [in] which the Milton Public Library is among the first in the State to try, and it is undertaken only after a year's study and investigation on the part of the Executive Committee, instigated from time to time by Mr. Clayton of the Board of Trustees."

In 1901, when the bookmobile concept was being investigated and further prompted by Helm Clayton, the trustees of the Milton Public Library then serving were Reverend Albert K. Teele, Edwin Dexter Wadsworth, Amor L. Hollingsworth, Orrin A. Andrews, Joseph Cutler Whitney, Reverend Roderick Stebbins, Nathaniel Thayer Kidder, Harrison Otis Apthorp, Charles E. Rogerson and H. Helm Clayton; the librarians were Gertrude Forrest at the Main Branch and Josephine Babcock in the East Milton Branch. With a town population of 6,809 residents, the circulation of the books amounted to 42,264

The horse-drawn Bookmobile of the Milton Public Library was established in 1902 and is thought to be the first of its kind in the United States. Ernest Leavitt and Frank Farrington stand with the horse-drawn delivery wagon behind the Milton Public Library about 1910, awaiting books that would be distributed from house to house in Milton. *Courtesy of the Milton Public Library.*

books in 1901, with an increase after the delivery service was implemented to 48,896 in 1902. This statistic allows an increase of 6.2 books to 7.2 books per person annually, so the perceived importance of the library was more than obvious. These trustees and the library staff realized that the traditional lending aspects of a library could be augmented by this "newfangled idea."

The bookmobile was to begin its service to town residents on January 2, 1902, with Frank H. Farrington on the book wagon. Books were to be delivered in the Blue Hill and Brush Hill districts every Tuesday and Wednesday. The delivery service was made possible "by the income of a fund left by Governor Wolcott for that purpose." With delivery service primarily directed toward the southwest part of town, the circulation of library books increased dramatically, and Mr. Farrington and his devoted nag plodded the streets of Milton, allowing patrons to browse the few shelves of books in the rear of the wagon that were protected by canvas tarps. This suitable

Milton Village, looking along Adams Street toward the Neponset River, was a mill village with residences and mills clustered along the river and surrounding streets. The Associates Building, the large brick building on the right, was designed by Rotch & Tilden and built in 1884. Here was located the Milton Public Library until it moved in 1904 to the new library designed by Shepley, Rutan and Coolidge at Canton Avenue and Reedsdale Road.

arrangement would continue unimpeded until January 27, 1927, when an unfortunate accident occurred when an automobile crashed into the horse-drawn bookmobile, destroying the wagon, scattering the books and severely injuring the horse, which had to be put down. Mr. Farrington, who had been operating the bookmobile since 1902, was reassigned to the library on Canton Avenue, where he assisted in the maintenance of the building. For a short period of time, Ernest E. Leavitt, superintendent of the library's building and grounds, operated a new bookmobile in a rented automobile until 1929; Mr. Leavitt later added makeshift bookcases in the rear of his own automobile, "covering the house-to-house system and expressed in much less time than the horse-drawn vehicle. The circulation at once increased."

Well, library bookmobiles are not quite as common as they were sixty years ago due to the increased use of the automobile; however, there is a strong probability that the Milton Public Library's house-to-house delivery of books by a horse-drawn wagon in 1902 might possibly be among the first, if not the first, instance of mobile book delivery in the United States.

HENDRIE'S DAIRY BAR

Hendrie's Dairy Bar was opened in 1940 in Edward T. O'Neill Square, at the junction of Central Avenue and Eliot Street. The former Bent's Cracker Factory at 131 Eliot Street was completely remodeled for the manufacture of Hendrie's Ice Cream, which later became this popular dairy bar that served delicious ice cream and sandwiches.

Hendrie's Ice Cream, said to have been "a favorite with the people of the community," was founded in 1885 and became a well-known caterer that provided delicious ice creams for receptions. The company, originally located near Franklin Field in Dorchester, had long been famous for the high-quality ice creams produced by the family and for its unparalleled service; however, that company was closed in 1925. The name "Hendries" had been so well known for four decades that it was revived in 1930 as the Eliot Creamery, Inc., Manufacturers of Hendrie's Ice Cream at 131 Eliot Street in Milton. It was said in 1947 that the "fact that the name Hendrie's had been associated with quality ice cream and high grade catering for so many years, it immediately began to flourish again, and has continued so that today it is one of New England's largest, independent ice cream manufacturers." The company

Hendrie's Dairy Bar was at Edward T. O'Neill Square, the junction of Central Avenue and Eliot Street. The building had been remodeled from the old Bent's Cracker Factory, and here patrons came for delicious ice cream and sandwiches. *Author's collection.*

was sold to White Brothers Creamery, which instituted changes such as the popular Hendrie's Dairy Bar. White Brothers had been located in the Atlantic section of Quincy and was one of numerous milk companies of the time, such as the Milton Hill Dairy owned by Michael W. Murray, the Sias Dairy Farm on Sias Lane and the Thatcher Farm on Thacher Street owned by Martin J. Manning, which had long delivered its "Creamy Milk" throughout the area.

The Eliot Street operation featured White Brothers milk, cream and dairy products. With the opening of the Dairy Bar, Hendrie's began offering a "varied and selected menu [which] includes breakfast, luncheon and dinner specials as well as sandwiches, ice cream and dairy drinks. A modern dairy bar, utilizing the very latest innovations in design and equipment, is one of the many features." This popular spot was reached by two levels of stone terraces and a winding stone walkway from the parking lot to the door. The grounds were attractively landscaped and greatly added to the square, which could be seen from the tables shaded by umbrellas in the summer months.

The building, which has been vacant for many years, has been slated for a development of condominiums in the near future.

MILTON VILLAGE, 1941

Seen in the accompanying photograph, Eleanor Kuppens selects evergreen spays from a display in front of the Milton Flower Shop. The shop was located on the left side of 71 Adams Street, the Milton Professional Building. Milton Village a half century ago had numerous businesses that attracted walk-in customers. Among them on the even side of Adams Street was the Milton Savings Bank (#40), the Milton Hill Pharmacy (#50), Holden's Hardware Store (#54), the Milton Record (#60) and Roulston Printers (#62); on the opposite side was the Norfolk County Trust Company, the Milton Village Jenney Service Station, the Thoms Dress Shop, the Milton Hill Beauty Shop (both #73), the Milton Flower Shop, Preston's Market (#75) and Fasch Studios (#95). This block on Adams Street, between Eliot Street and Canton Avenue, has gone through many changes, but never more so than in the twentieth century.

Beginning at the corner of Eliot Street was the Blue Hills Trust Company, later the Norfolk County Trust Company and now Bank of America, after a multitude of intervening names. Designed by Milton architect Arthur Wallace Rice and built in 1929, it is an impressive red brick Colonial Revival bank with distinctive interior wood paneling and furniture made for the bank. Adjacent to it was the Livery Stable of Lemuel Crossman, three stories on Adams Street and two stories on High Street, where horses were boarded, groomed and shod; it was destroyed by fire in 1953 and is now a parking area for the bank. Adjacent to it was the Phineas Paine House, built circa 1805, which later became the site of a Jenney Service Station and is now the Citizens Bank drive-through. Next door at 71 Adams Street is the Milton Professional Building. Built in 1765 by Joseph Fenno, is the oldest building in Milton Village, though it has undergone tremendous changes through renovations and new exterior siding. Number 75 Adams Street is a two-story suite of professional offices that was formerly Preston's Market. It was built on the site of the home and shop of Benjamin Crehore, who made pianofortes and bass viols. The Therese Marie Photo Studio, set high above a stone retaining wall, is the former Baker Building, owned by Edmund J. Baker; it was across the street facing Wharf Street and was moved when the Associates Building was built. At the corner of Canton Avenue was the old Rising Sun Tavern, a colonial hostelry that served potent libations as well as providing a

Eleanor Kuppens arranges flowers in front of the Milton Flower Shop on Adams Street in Milton Village in 1941.

comfortable bed for weary travelers on the old Plymouth Highway. Today, it is the site of the Chapman, Cole & Gleason Funeral Home.

In the distance can be seen the Administration Building of the Baker Chocolate Company, designed and built in 1919 by Milton architect George F. Shepard Jr. of the Boston architectural firm of Shepard & Stearns; this impressive Classical Revival building has recently been remodeled for artists' lofts, along with the preservation of its great neon sign surmounting the roof. To the right is a corner of the Bispham Block, designed by Dorchester architect Joseph Tilden Greene. Looming above the storefronts on Dorchester Avenue is the Gilbert Stuart School, which was a public elementary school built in 1909 by the City of Boston on Richmond Street. It is now the site of the Lower Mills Branch of the Boston Public Library.

Chapter 5

PLACES OF EDUCATION

THE FIRST MILTON HIGH SCHOOL

The old Milton Academy building once stood at the crest of Academy Hill, the area of Milton Centre now occupied by the Milton Town Hall and the Central Fire House. In 1866, the academy suspended its charter and leased the building to the Town of Milton for use as its first public high school, which had recently been founded.

In the nineteenth century, the Commonwealth of Massachusetts had enacted support for local high schools, and in 1866 the town meeting accepted the financial support and established a public high school. Sereno D. Hunt was the sole teacher for the three-year course with "an average of 44 students for the summer term and 34 for the winter term." The old academy building, which was built by William B. Crehore in 1807, was "two stories high, with a porch at the end, together with the necessary out-buildings and fences." It was set on a forty-two-acre tract of land purchased by Edward Hutchinson Robbins and donated to the new academy, which had been founded in 1798. Throughout the years, the academy had "been suspended for short periods, only to rise again into new life"; however, in 1866, upon the establishment of a public high school in Milton "free to all its youth," the academy was suspended and the building was leased to the town until 1880.

The first Milton High School was in the former Milton Academy Building on Academy Hill, at Canton Avenue and Thatcher Street. Built by William B. Crehore in 1807, it was originally used by Milton Academy until it suspended its charter in 1866, after which it was used as the town high school until 1885. *Author's collection.*

The Milton High School was headed by Mr. Hunt, the former principal of Milton Academy, who was selected by the town to lead the new public high school. Mr. Hunt served as headmaster for eleven years, after which he was succeeded by W.E. Bunten and Hiram Tuell. The high school continued with various teachers, including unmarried female assistants (one had to resign if she married) and teachers in drawing, music and sewing. Open to all and remarkably able to function on the percentage earmarked from the tax base, the first Milton High School served as a fledgling institution that grew haphazardly in leased property until 1885, when the Town of Milton voted an appropriation to build a new high school, which was built on nearly the same site as the old academy building. Designed by Arthur Rotch and George T. Tilden of the Boston architectural firm of Rotch & Tilden, the new Milton High School was a brick, two-story building entered by a Romanesque arch with a flight of stairs. The school was eighty-four feet long and fifty feet wide and had schoolrooms, recitation rooms, a teachers' room and two laboratories (one chemical and the other physical) on the second floor, which was shared by an exercise room, all of which were modernly "ventilated into a large brick shaft, through which passes the iron smokepipe from the furnaces."

The large and commodious high school designed by local architect Bradford O. Hamilton and built in 1895 on Engine Street all but enveloped

The second Milton High School was designed by the noted architectural firm of Rotch & Tilden and built in 1885. A large addition was added in 1895 and designed by local architect Bradford O. Hamilton. In 1917, it became the Vose School and was used as an elementary school until its demolition in 1956. *Author's collection.*

the 1885 building, which had its entrance and façade incorporated as the center core of the new building. The curriculum had been widely expanded since 1866 and, by the turn of the twentieth century, offered various courses for students, including college, business and general courses of study. The first Milton High School was a far cry from the school of today, but they both offer a high-quality education in Milton "free to all its youth."

THE SCHOOL FOR WHICH SCHOOL STREET WAS NAMED

I think School Street, which runs from Randolph Avenue to Central Avenue, is an attractive residential street, but where is the school? Obviously, if it was so named it should have a school on the street, but the closest one is the Glover School on Canton Avenue. What gives here?

Well, School Street was actually laid out in 1848 by John Murray Forbes (1813–1898) on a tract of land he had purchased in 1842 at the auction of Dr. Amos Holbrook's estate; laid out between Randolph and Canton Avenues, it was originally known as Glover Street. The North District School, later to be

Students, along with their teacher, pose in 1885 on the steps of the Center School. Located on Canton Avenue, between Wendell Park and Thatcher Street, it was typical of the mid-nineteenth-century schoolhouses built in Milton. At that time there was the East School on Adams Street, the West School on Blue Hill Avenue, the North School on School Street and the Center School on Canton Avenue.

renamed the Glover School in memory of early landowner and farmer John Glover (d. 1653), was on a lot donated to the town by Mr. Forbes in exchange for the old school lot on Milton Hill. The school was to be built here after a fire in 1846 had destroyed the old North School, which was located on what is now Hutchinson Field on Milton Hill. The school's presence on the elm-shaded street eventually led to the renaming of the street after the school, which upon completion was called "very commodious" in the annual town report. Seen in the accompanying photograph, circa 1885, students of the coeducational North School pose on the steep steps of the school along with Clarence Boylston, schoolmaster from 1880 to 1887, who is seen in the rear row, third from the left.

The North District School, one of six mid-nineteenth-century schools throughout the town, was a late Greek Revival two-story wood-framed building with flat corner pilasters and a small center portico. A steep flight of steps (still to be seen at the right of the driveway at 150 School Street) led to the entrance. Used for just four decades, a new Glover School was built in 1888, sited at an angle to the street, and served the town until the present

Glover School, built on part of the extensive lands of John Glover, was built in 1950 on Canton Avenue adjacent to Turner's Pond.

Eventually, the Glover School proved too small to accommodate the students in the neighborhood, and the building was sold and moved to the northwest corner of Canton Avenue and School Street, where it was converted into a private residence. Today, the former Glover School still stands at 147 Canton Avenue, and though dramatically altered, it represents one of the earliest school buildings to remain in Milton.

OLD BRICK SCHOOL

The Old Brick School, or the Brush Hill School, was built in 1812 at the corner of Brush Hill Turnpike (now Blue Hill Avenue) and Atherton Street. A small one-story brick building, it had a colonnade of four Doric columns supporting a porch roof and a pedimented façade gable. Seen in

Jesse Pierce (1788–1856) was an educator at the Old Brick School, as were his brothers Joel and John Pierce. From 1819 to 1825, Pierce kept a private school on Canton Avenue, which was a feeder to Milton Academy. He was said to be "a man of strict integrity, high minded and honorable, and universally beloved and respected in all the various relations of life." His son, Edward Lillie Pierce, was to become president of the Baker Chocolate Company.

the accompanying photograph, students pose around the school in the mid-nineteenth century.

Among the early nineteenth-century teachers at this school were brothers Jesse, Joel and John Pierce, whose brother Otis Pierce also taught school in Milton at the Scotts Woods School; Jesse Pierce later opened a private school on Canton Avenue in Milton. The rudiments of teaching were undertaken in this one-room, coeducational primary school that operated from harvest time to early spring. The schoolteachers often boarded with families in the neighborhood, and they fared poorly considering the importance of their work in educating the youth of Milton. Students rarely went on to pursue further education, and if they did, it was at Milton Academy, for the Milton High School was not founded until 1866, after which the academy was suspended and the academy building was leased to the town for the new high school at Academy Hill.

The population in Milton during the nineteenth century had grown steadily since the "Old Brick" was built, and due to the increased population of the Brush Hill area due to the development of Fairmount Hill (the area

The Old Brick Schoolhouse was built in 1812 at the corner of Blue Hill Avenue and Atherton Street. Demolished in 1870 when the Sumner School was built on the site, it was later to become the site of the Atherton Street Fire Station.

between Brush Hill Road and the Neponset River), in 1857 the town built the Fairmount School, which was operated until 1868, when the Fairmount neighborhood of Milton was ceded to the new town of Hyde Park. The "Old Brick" was demolished in 1870, after which the Sumner School was built on its site. New names for the Milton schools were proposed by the Reverend Albert K. Teele, chairman of the Milton School Committee, who spoke before the citizens at town hall. He proposed the renaming of the "Old Brick" in honor of the Sumner family, headed by William Sumner (1604–1698) who owned extensive tracts of land in the Brush Hill area and was the ancestor of such prominent descendants as Governor Increase Sumner; his son William Hyslop Sumner, who developed East Boston and for whom the Sumner Tunnel was named; and Senator Charles Sumner, the great abolitionist. Reverend Teele said that by giving the Sumner "names to the schools of Milton…all our sons and daughters may well emulate" their "rare qualities of heart and mind."

The Blue Hill Hose Company, which was near the corner of Canton Avenue and Dollar Lane, was supplanted by Engine Firehouse #4, or the Atherton Street Firehouse, which was built in 1901 to serve the Brush Hill area of the town. The Sumner School and the firehouse were surrounded by the property of B.G.A. Rosentwist and Maria Oxton, whose husband was agent for the Eustis Estate, while just west on Blue Hill Avenue were the homes of the Martin and Byrnes families. Today, the site of the "Old Brick" School is occupied by Coulter Landscaping and Greenhouses.

Fresh Air Classes

Recently, I was reading a 1941 edition of the *Milton Record* newspaper and came across an intriguing reference to the "Fresh Air Classes" from the primary schools to the Cunningham Junior High School and the Milton High School. For the life of me I could not really understand what the fresh air classes represented or why they were instituted. In a photograph from 1939, which appeared in the *Boston Herald Traveler*, schoolchildren at the Collicott Elementary School on Edge Hill Road participated in an outdoor "School Siesta." The idea behind these breaks was to allow children to rest during the school day and, in cooler weather, to wear warm wool hooded ponchos as they relaxed on canvas cots. Now I must admit a nap sounds tempting, but for young, ever-energetic schoolchildren?

This 1941 article explained the success of the Fresh Air Work in the Milton Schools and stated that with donations from private sources, the school committee was able to "extend the work of the Fresh Air Rooms to the junior and senior high schools [from the elementary schools due to their success]. Superintendent of Milton schools Horace F. Turner reported the success of the classes and explained that with parental approval, "pupils may lie down for a period of time provided on their daily program, and later, refreshed, take up the remaining activities of the school day." The benefits of this class were said to be that the "conservation of strength while in attendance at school have far reaching effects upon both physical and mental health of some who could not stand the strain of full-time study and school activities."

Only a generation before, it would have been necessary for students to have convalesced at home after a serious illness or operation, while missing part of the scheduled school year and thereby seriously affecting their school progress. Under these fresh air classes, the schoolchildren could benefit from a nap in the fresh air and wake up refreshed and invigorated by healthy doses of sunshine and cool, fresh air.

Upon reflection, there must have really been something in it when our grandparents said we should go out onto the piazza for a "breath of fresh air."

Chapter 6

PLACES OF WORSHIP

THE CHURCH OF OUR SAVIOUR

The Church of Our Saviour, seen in the accompanying photograph from 1905, was established in East Milton as a mission of St. Michael's Episcopal Church. Designed by William Ralph Emerson (1833–1917), a Milton resident and noted architect who is considered the "Father of Shingle-Style Architecture," the English Gothic Perpendicular stucco and granite church was built at the corner of Adams and Babcock Streets.

The mission in East Milton was established in 1897 for those who wished to worship in an Anglican manner but not travel to St. Michael's Church on Randolph Avenue. The first services were held in Washington Hall in East Milton, which was at the corner of Granite Avenue and Mechanic Street; however, those early worshippers wanted a permanent church. The cornerstone, a granite stone inscribed "1903" in Roman numerals, was ceremoniously laid by Bishop William Lawrence, and the cost for the land and church was received from "members of the Mission through pledges, offerings and annual fairs. The people as a whole have not solicited money from outsiders, believing the respect of the community for the church and its work would be best gained by showing a tendency to carry their Church of Saviour on Adams Street own burdens." Though a mission of St. Michael's (of which it would remain until 1923), the "Mission Church of Our Savior" was to become a thriving parish after August 1904, when the first service

The Church of Our Saviour is at the corner of Adams and Babcock Streets. Opened in 1897 as a mission of St. Michael's Church, the church was designed by William Ralph Emerson and built in 1903 in the English Gothic Perpendicular style. *Author's collection.*

was held and the church dedicated. As the *Milton Record* stated in its August 27, 1904 edition, the church is "built in the [English] perpendicular style of Gothic architecture, with a granite base, and walls of stone colored plaster. The inside woodwork, except the floor which is finished in natural color, is dark brown, and the plaster is pleasing stone green. The present building represents only part of the nave as the future choir is planned." With seating for 175 worshippers, the mission was established to serve many of those whose livelihoods were derived from the granite industry in Quincy and East Milton.

In 1914, the church was consecrated to the Glory of God, as the mortgage had been paid by the parishioners. In 1924, the church was lengthened by one bay to five bays in the rear, with accommodations for a choir with stalls. Entered through a porch of hewn wood trusses supporting a gable roof of wood shingles, the impression that the church gives is one of an English village church. The church has an important baptismal font, which has a stone incorporated into its overall design, as the top stone; this was received from Milton Abbey in Milton Abbas, England, upon the request in 1904 by Reverend T.I. Reece when he preached at both Milton Abbey and St. Catherine's Chapel in the Milton Abbey grounds. Founded in AD 938, the ancient abbey was built prior to the Norman Conquest and has been rebuilt and added to over the last millennium. This stone and another given to St. Michael's Church—which, ironically, was a patron saint of the Milton Abbey and the St. Catherine's Guild—signify a bond between the two Miltons. The church was built in what was then more of a residential neighborhood, with the Hutchinson Brackett House on the left and the Sheldon House across the street. Seen in the photograph, the now extensively remodeled house on the left was built about 1840 by Daniel Hutchinson, a granite worker, and was later occupied by Elmer Brackett (1866–1947), a noted inventor. Mr. Brackett invented the granite polishing wheel that allowed granite to be polished to a smooth, mirror-like shine; he also invented a machine to produce carbon paper, a time-saving invention that revolutionized office work a century ago. On the far left can be seen the Italianate façade of the Dr. Philip Foisie House at 487 Adams Street, now the law offices of Robert Jubinville, Esq.

St. Agatha Church

St. Agatha Church was the first Roman Catholic church to be built in Milton, and it was completed in 1935. Originally, Roman Catholics in Milton had attended St. Gregory's Church on Dorchester Avenue in Dorchester Lower Mills after its founding in 1863, and Milton Hill up to School Street remains within the parish today. However, in 1917, a small chapel for worship as a mission of St. Gregory's Church was erected on Adams Street in East Milton and was consecrated to St. Agatha when the parish was created in 1922.

The parish of St. Agatha was headed by Father Eugene Carney, who served as rector for the next twenty-five years. It was under his direction that the present church was begun on the former Babcock Estate; it was designed by Milton architect Alexander J. Scholtes (1880–1948). Scholtes was a parishioner of St. Agatha Church and a resident of 48 Pierce Street in East Milton; he was also an accomplished architect whose designs for an impressive Modern Gothic stone church must have greatly pleased parishioners. St. Agatha Church was to be built on Adams Street opposite Brook Road and was designed as a cruciform church with an imposing battlement tower on the façade, which had sandstone Gothic pinnacles soaring high above the crenellated tower. Mr. Scholtes was a 1903 graduate of the Massachusetts Institute of Technology and had both a private architectural practice as well as that of consulting architect with the prestigious Olmsted Associates of

Brookline—which had been founded by the premier landscape architect Frederick Law Olmsted—for four decades. In designing the church, Mr. Scholtes strategically placed the church directly at the lot edge on Adams Street, and the seven-bay church, still the largest in Milton, can be prominently seen as one approaches from all three directions. Mr. Scholtes was an associate professor of architecture at MIT from 1920 to 1922, which was the oldest school of architecture in the United States. Founded in 1865 by William R. Ware (1832–1915) of Milton Hill, this school would train the first generation of American architects rather than seeing them educated abroad at L'Ecole des Beaux-Arts in Paris. Scholtes also taught at the Lothrop School in Groton. When he began his own practice in Boston, he combined his skills as an architect with the study of landscape architecture. Not well known, nor is there a concise listing of his architectural commissions, he did design a remarkably impressive parish church that was built of locally quarried granite with sandstone stringcourses, window surrounds and tower crenellation. Eventually, the parish campus was to include a parochial school designed by Joseph McGann and built in 1950 and a brick rectory designed by Thomas H. Fallon & Sons and built in 1958, which today creates a unified plan that dominates this area of East Milton.

St. Agatha Church was designed by Alexander J. Scholtes (1880–1948) and completed in 1935 on Adams Street in East Milton. A Modern Gothic stone church, it has an imposing battlement tower on the façade and soaring sandstone Gothic pinnacles. *Author's collection.*

St. Michael's Church

St. Michael's Church was built in 1898 in the "early English style of architecture" of rough coursed granite blocks set in a random ashlar design. Built in "one of the most beautiful suburbs of Boston" on Randolph Avenue within an impressive residential area, the church was set on a portion of the former Governor Hutchinson–Barney Smith–Jonathan Russell Estate. The church was the first Episcopal church in Milton, and its design and setting emulated that of an English village church.

St. Michael's Church was designed by Ralph Lincoln Emerson (1868–1899) and built in 1898 on Randolph Avenue. The church was later enlarged by Ralph Adams Cram in 1916, with a Tudor Revival half-timbered parish house being built adjacent to the church. *Author's collection.*

In 1895, the Gannett, Herrick, Hollis, Jackson, Lee, Reynolds, Whitney and Wilde families requested that Episcopal services be held at Fraternity Hall, the third-floor assembly hall in the Associates Building in Milton Village. Previously, those seeking to attend worship might go to St. Mary's or All Saints Churches in Dorchester, the Church of the Holy Spirit in Mattapan or Christ Church in Quincy. From that time until 1898, the Episcopal Mission in Milton served the needs of the community. With the laying of the cornerstone bearing the signs of the Alpha and the Omega in 1898, the simple but impressive design was that of Ralph Lincoln Emerson (1868–1899), a young architect who lived across the street. Son of the noted architect William Ralph Emerson (1833–1917), who is considered the "Father of Shingle-style" architecture, Ralph was graduated from Harvard College in 1891, after which he served as a draftsman in his father's architectural office until his untimely death in 1899. A promising architect, Ralph L. Emerson was a friend of Ralph Adams Cram, a draftsman in the architectural firm of Rotch & Tilden. Arthur Rotch and William T. Tilden were partners who would eventually, with his partner Ferguson, design the Parish House that was built adjacent to the church in 1911.

St. Michael's originally consisted of only a nave and small chancel. Built for a suburban town, the parish consisted of a "community of well-to-do people" with a seating capacity of two hundred people. The church, with its asymmetrical stone tower that also served as the lancet-arched entrance, was to receive in 1904 a piece of stone from the Milton Abbey in Milton Abbas, England. At the request of Reverend Theodore I. Reece—who served as first lay reader and rector from 1898 to 1907, after which he served as bishop of southwestern Ohio—a piece of the Norman abbey was sent to Milton, where it was incorporated as a historically associated keystone over the inner entrance of St. Michael's Church.

As the parish increased in size, a Tudor Revival half-timbered Parish House, with stucco emulating Medieval wattle and daub, was built in 1911. The chancel of the church was further enlarged in 1916 with an impressive stained-glass window designed by Ralph Adams Cram that was placed above the John Evans–designed altar. It is thought that the rectory of St. Michael's Church, which was built in 1898, was also designed by Ralph Lincoln Emerson. A substantial asymmetrical Shingle-style house with a sloping shed-like dormered roof in the style of William Ralph Emerson, the

Young choir members process from the Children's Church after a Christmas service in 1945. The Children's Church was originally a school built in 1844; it was moved in 1937 and remodeled by Eliot Putnam of Putnam & Cox and is adjacent to the First Parish Church in Milton, Unitarian. The services are only for children and are conducted by themselves. *Author's collection.*

rectory was originally built closer to the church on the present site of the driveway and was moved to its present location in 1953.

Sadly, St. Michael's Church and the rectory are among the few designs of Ralph Lincoln Emerson to have been built. In 1899, he married Lillias Stephenson, daughter of Colonel Stephenson of Milton, but he died the next day. So ended what was ultimately destined to be a brilliant architectural career.

Chapter 7

STREETS, ESTATES AND SITES

CUNNINGHAM PARK

Edward Cunningham (1823–1889) was a partner in the firm of Russell & Company, a noted China trade firm that traded in the Far East in the mid-nineteenth century. A member of a well-connected seafaring family with close relations to other China trade families in Milton, he lived in China until 1857, when he returned to Milton with a fortune derived from the Chinese trade and purchased a large estate in East Milton.

Cunningham acquired 150 acres of land on both sides of Edge Hill Road and, in 1871, built an impressive stone and wood Stick-style mansion. The mansion was primarily built of granite, according to a short history written by his daughter Hester Cunningham, that was "from the upper surface of the quarry" adjacent to the property in Quincy. Mr. Cunningham and his wife, Frances Handasyd Cary Cunningham (1832–1889), lived a comfortable life on their estate and kept a summer house on Brush Isle off the Cohasset coast. In recognition of his China trade connections, and from which his vast fortune was derived, he often flew a red and yellow Chinese flag when in residence. The Milton estate was embellished with large stone "Lions of Buddha" carved from a "conglomerate stone" in the Shanghai area of China, each weighing 2,500 pounds; these flanked the entrance to the estate. A large bronze temple bell with Chinese characters was brought from Shanghai, China, to Milton in 1870 and was reputedly cast in 1656,

Edward Cunningham (1823–1889) was a partner in the firm of Russell & Company, a noted China trade firm. He lived in China until just prior to the Civil War, when he returned and purchased 150 acres in Milton, where he built a large stone mansion. *Courtesy of Edith Cunningham Crocker.*

the "13th year of Shunchi," with copper coins from the inhabitants of Shanghai. The bell weighs 1,335 pounds and is presently on the grounds of the Captain Robert Bennet Forbes House on Milton Hill. Mr. Cunningham was also a collector of fine Chinese art and jade carvings, which were used throughout the house, imparting an exotic and unique atmosphere.

He was not to enjoy his estate for long, as he was unfortunately shot in 1889 by a wood poacher on his estate and subsequently died of his wound. In 1904, Mrs. Edward Cunningham sold a portion of the estate to Charles Davis, whose twenty-acre estate on Pleasant Street was henceforth known as Carmarthen, and a large portion to the trustees of the Cunningham Estate. Edward Cunningham's aunt was Mary Abbot Forbes Cunningham

(1814–1904), the widow of the Reverend Francis Cunningham and sister of John Murray Forbes and Robert Bennet Forbes. Upon her death, Mrs. Cunningham bequeathed her fortune to three trustees—Malcolm Forbes, Nathaniel F. Stone and Thomas Nelson Perkins—and stated that it was to be used to benefit the residents of Milton. The trustees purchased a large portion of the Cunningham Estate in East Milton, including the mansion, after which Frances Cary Cunningham built a Shingle-style house at 175 Edge Hill Road on an eight-acre remnant of the vast estate. This was later owned by Jesse Bunton Baxter, superintendent of Cunningham Park, as the former estate became known (this is now the site of the community gardens). Living in the neighborhood were her children: Ethel Cunningham Cabot,

Emma Forbes Ware (1838–1898) founded the Milton Convalescent Home in 1887 at the corner of Canton Avenue and Thatcher Street. Miss Ware was steadfast in soliciting financial support and interest for her home, where patients recuperating from surgery or illness had a place of quiet convalescence. *Private collection.*

wife of Francis Elliot Cabot, whose thirteen-acre estate was near Edge Hill Road on Cedar Road; Hester and Hilda Cunningham, who lived with their mother until her death, after which Hilda married Paul Connor; and Edward Jr., who married Edith Perkins Cunningham and lived in Boston's Back Bay and Westwood.

In 1904, the mansion was offered to the Milton Convalescent Home by the trustees of the Cunningham Estate as a new and more convenient location; the home had been founded by Emma Ware Forbes (1838–1898) in 1887 at the corner of Canton Avenue and Thacher Street. The Milton Convalescent Home readily adapted to the former Cunningham Mansion, and the first superintendent was Miss O'Brien. The former mansion had bedrooms now being used as wards for patients, and the stone tower above the entrance became the nurses' quarters.

What was once a comfortable family home had now become a place of convalescence for those recuperating from surgery or illness, with extensive landscaped grounds and the remnants of formal gardens. The patients' recovery at the convalescent home must have been enhanced by the setting.

The Milton Youth Group often sponsored dances at Cunningham Park Hall, which brought together young adults for an enjoyable evening. Seen here in 1958, young Miltonians are on the dance floor enjoying the latest dance craze. *Author's collection.*

THE CARY ESTATE

The Cary Mansion was on Adams Street just north of Squantum Street and was a large wood-framed Italianate house that was enlarged over the years. It was owned by Edward M. Cary (1828–1888) and Alice Hathaway Forbes Cary (1838–1917), who had married in 1875. The twenty-acre estate was flanked on the north by the Cornelius Babcock Estate (later to become the Bowditch Estate, which was known as Eastover and whose carriage drive is perpetuated by Father Carney Drive) and on the south by the Bass Estate, which was ten acres adjacent to Squantum Street. Edward Cary was the son of Helen Paine and George B. Cary (1792–1880) who came to Milton to

The Cary Mansion was built by Edward Cary (1828–1888) and Alice Forbes Cary (1838–1917) and was a ten-acre estate off Adams Street at the foot of Milton Hill. The estate was developed by the Cary Hill Realty Company, and Cabot Street and Cary Avenue were laid out with large one-family houses built in the subdivision. *Courtesy of Edith Cunningham Crocker.*

become president of the Granite Railway Company, serving from 1833 to 1853. He was the nephew of Colonel Thomas H. Perkins, the first president and promoter of the Granite Railway Company and popularly known as the "Merchant Prince of Boston," in addition to having been honored by the naming of the Perkins School for the Blind. Alice Cary was the daughter of John Murray Forbes and Sarah Swain Hathaway Forbes, whose estate was known as Fredonia. Cary Mansion was just south of their property. The Carys, who were childless, laid out a magnificent estate that had a curvilinear drive that is today perpetuated by Cary Avenue and Cabot Street.

THE PINES: THE KENNEDY ESTATE

Recently, I visited my friend Helen Buchanan at Fuller Village. As I entered the driveway, I was amazed at the impressive buildings known as Depoyan House and Foster House and the lush green lawns and newly planted trees. As I entered the lobby, I was equally impressed with the elegant interiors but more than satisfied that the Milton Residences for the Elderly (MRE) had decided to save the old Kennedy House and restore it as part of the village.

The Kennedy House was built as a summer house about 1878 and known as the Pines. Set on a sixty-one-acre estate that had been landscaped by the noted firm of Olmsted Associates, the successors to Frederick Law Olmsted, the estate is at the corner of Blue Hill Avenue and Brush Hill Road. Dr. George Golding Kennedy (1841–1918) was a noted physician who was graduated from Harvard College and the Harvard Medical School. In 1867, he assumed control of the establishment of Kennedy's Medical Discovery, which had been founded by his father, Donald Kennedy (1812–1909), a native of Glenmoritson, Scotland.

Dr. Donald Kennedy had begun the manufacture and sale of his "celebrated medical compound…in a very humble way, carrying it around in a carpet-bag" through his hometown of Roxbury and, later, Boston. It was said that in the "judicious manner in which the 'Discovery' was placed before the public, together with the intrinsic merit of the article itself, soon made his name well known throughout the civilized world." Following in the success of his father in the widespread distribution of "Kennedy's Medical Discovery"—which the author assumed was similar to other medicines marketed at that time that contained a liberal dose of

Fuller Village is operated by the Milton Residences for the Elderly on the former Kennedy Estate at Blue Hill Avenue and Brush Hill Road. Incorporating the former mansion, the complex sprawls on either side of the main entrance and fulfills the desire of Caroline Weld Fuller (1863–1931) to provide a safe and secure place of residence for the elderly. *Author's collection.*

alcohol and herbs—Dr. George G. Kennedy continued its manufacture in Roxbury until he moved from Roxbury to Milton full time sometime after 1892. With a liberal income derived from the "Discovery," Dr. Kennedy indulged his passion for the study of botany at the Pines. Once a student of the celebrated Professor Asa Gray of Harvard, Dr. Kennedy had gone on to found the New England Botanical Club, specializing in the plant life deciduous to New England. He also served on the Visiting Committee of the Gray Herbarium at Harvard, where a bronze tablet was erected in his honor in 1915. As a frequent contributor to *Rhodora*, the journal of the New England Botanical Club, he wrote on his interests pertaining to botany and herbiculture, much of which took place in Milton.

Upon Dr. Kennedy's death, the estate was inherited by his son, Dr. Harris Kennedy (1871–1938), a specialist in the study of infant paralysis who at one time served as chairman of the Milton School Committee and as president of both the Milton Educational Society and the Milton Historical Society.

The gardens at the Pines, the Kennedy Estate on Blue Hill Avenue, were superbly planted. Laid out by Frederick Law Olmsted, the estate was greatly enhanced by George and Frances Keene Kennedy, who cultivated over fifty varieties of the *Iris Kampferi*, arranged in the Japanese manner with a wood bridge and numerous lanterns. *Author's collection.*

Dr. Kennedy and his wife, Frances Keene Kennedy, expanded the gardens at the Pines to include Japanese iris, of which they became well known as noted hyridizers. With over fifty varieties of the *Iris Kampferi* being cultivated in their garden, the Kennedys created a noteworthy garden that was later arranged in the Japanese manner with a Japanese teahouse, a pagoda and garden accessories. So authentic was this garden that the Kennedys often dressed in kimonos and strung Japanese lanterns to illuminate the garden in the evening. The estate was often used for fundraising purposes and was the scene of lavish garden parties, among them one in honor of Japan's victory over Russia in 1905 and another for members of the Japanese Parliament in 1921. Mrs. Kennedy also held annual parties for the benefit of Radcliffe College, of which she was an alumna.

In 1933, Dr. Kennedy sold thirty acres of the estate to the Fuller Trust Inc., a benevolent organization that had been established by Caroline Weld Fuller (1863–1931). The house was converted to a retirement home, providing "the comforts and care of a home for homeless women of refinement who for one reason or another found themselves invalid, penniless, or unhappy." Miss Fuller had been crippled at a young age in a riding accident and thereafter confined to a hotel suite at the Hotel Vendome in Boston's Back Bay. It was her idea that the home should retain all of the feeling of a private residence and avoid the appearance of an institution. Her bequest was known as the Fuller Trust, a charitable home that opened in 1934 with twelve female residents. Today, under the able direction of the MRE, the property has become Fuller Village.

THE ELIOT MEMORIAL BRIDGE

Charles Eliot was associated with the Olmsted Associates, the successor firm to Frederick Law Olmsted, the first professional landscape architect in the United States, and was justifiably called the "Father of the Metropolitan Park Commission."

Son of Charles W. Eliot (president of Harvard University from 1869 to 1909) and Grace Hopkinson Eliot, Charles Eliot (1859–1897) was graduated from Harvard in 1882, after which he studied landscape architecture at the Bussey Institute of the Arnold Arboretum. A well-respected environmentalist and the first landscape architect to work on the development of the park system, he successfully urged the incorporation of the Massachusetts Trustees of Public Reservations in 1891 and the Metropolitan Park Commission a year later. He joined with Frederick Law Olmsted and John C. Olmsted in 1893 to form the firm of Olmsted, Olmsted & Eliot, which was then employed by the Metropolitan Commission as landscape architects. An astute conservationist, advocate for public enjoyment and ardent proponent of the preservation of open lands, Eliot's vision included a virtual greenbelt surrounding Boston, with the Blue Hills Reservation being incorporated to protect the Great Blue Hill, the lesser hills and the surrounding lands. His chief virtues were thought to be simplicity and steadfastness, but his visionary plans of connected green spaces on the outskirts of the metropolitan area were to continue the establishment of national parks, forests and reserves like the Yellowstone National Park, which was the first to be established in the United States in 1872.

Eliot married Mary Yale Pitkin, and they lived on Brush Hill Road in Milton. Their four daughters were Ruth (Mrs. Roger Pierce of Milton),

The Eliot Memorial Bridge was erected in 1904 in memory of Charles Eliot (1859–1897), a principal in the landscape architectural firm of Olmsted, Olmsted & Eliot. Eliot was responsible for the Metropolitan Park Commission and the trustees of Public Reservations. His early death was commemorated by a rustic stone bridge in the Blue Hills, designed by Alexander Wadsworth Longfellow. *Author's collection.*

Grace (Mrs. W. Perry Dudley), Ellen (Mrs. Richard Paine) and Carola (Mrs. Lev Goriansky). Charles Eliot died young, at the age of thirty-seven, and as a fitting memorial to him, a stone bridge was proposed to be designed and built in the Blue Hill Reservation. It was said that "there seems a peculiar fitness in placing the memorial bridge—a tribute from his classmates and friends—in the great Blue Hills reservation of four thousand seven hundred acres, a region which engaged his best efforts."

Erected in 1904, the sturdy bridge of "simplicity and steadfastness" was designed by the Olmsted Brothers, his former business associates. Alexander Wadsworth Longfellow acted as advisory architect, and C.R. Harley designed the bronze tablet. The seventy-foot bridge of rough split stone secured on the edge of the hilltop and the five-foot-wide path spanned "a deep gully in the side of the hill...and is substantially built of heavy boulders and capped with granite blocks." The "views are as good from points just below the hilltop, along the rim of rock lying just above the scrub growth which clothes the upper flanks." Viewed from the bridge is "the sunny Marigold Valley, probably the most retired and peaceful spot in the metropolitan district."

The inscription on the tablet reads:

> *This bridge was erected in 1904 in memory of Charles Eliot, landscape architect to the Metropolitan Park Commission. By ample knowledge, intelligent perseverance and eloquent teaching, he created and inspired organizations capable of accomplishing his great purpose, the preservation of our historical and beautiful places.*

A true visionary cut short in the prime of his life, Charles Eliot was not only to be remembered for this memorial bridge, "part of the roughness and mass of the hilltop, a beautiful feature and a lasting memorial" that was to be held in perpetuity for public use and enjoyment, but also for the first course in landscape architecture, which was endowed in his name at Harvard University in 1900. Though the Blue Hill Observatory caps the 635-foot Great Blue Hill and offers superb panoramic views from its lofty vantage point, the Eliot Memorial Bridge serves as a reminder of the man whose efforts secured the land that is enjoyed by his fellow Miltonians a century after his death.

THE GULLIVER ELM

The Gulliver Elm once stood on Canton Avenue, adjacent to the town pound. The majestic elm tree had a fourteen-foot, four-inch trunk and stood between Elm and Gulliver Streets.

The town pound, a stone-walled enclosure for animals, was relocated in 1774 to Canton Avenue opposite Holmes Lane. The pound, the fourth in the town's history, had both cattle and swine placed in the enclosure rather than being allowed to roam the town streets. The pound was built on ministerial lands owned by the Milton Meetinghouse, opposite the house of Benjamin Read, a pump-maker that was at the lane leading to the house of Joseph Holman, for whom Holman Lane was named. The girth of the Gulliver elm was so great that its roots had encroached upon the sidewalk. Saved once from destruction, it was again considered a public hindrance and was

The Gulliver Elm was a massive tree on Canton Avenue, adjacent to the town pound. The tree had a fourteen-foot, four-inch trunk and was thought so important that it was deeded in 1833 to Isaac Gulliver by the First Congregational Church for preservation and "perpetual exemption from molestation." Today, Gulliver and Elm Streets perpetuate this once magnificent tree.

scheduled to be cut down. According to Teele's *History of Milton*, the fate of the condemned tree was quickly determined when "Miss Polly Vose…living in the house-opposite, heard the first blow of the axe, and presented herself to remonstrate. The men replied, 'We must obey orders,' and began again to ply their axes. She hurried back to the house and returned with a mug of cider, thus addressing the men; 'Come, now, take a drink of cider, and do just wait till I can see the selectmen.' They drank the cider, shouldered their axes, and went off." Miss Vose was obviously a woman not to cross, even by the town selectmen, and her mug of hard cider "took the edge off" the woodsmen's determination and the sharpness of their axe.

Saved for the time being, the tree would become a graceful addition to the town and was to be protected by a joint agreement between the First Congregational Church in Milton and Isaac Gulliver, who was bonded to preserve the elm tree. If ever the "said tree should decay, and from a ruinous state no longer continue to afford the shade and ornament desired by the Parish Society, that then it may and shall be at my disposal, without any let or hindrance on the part and behalf of said first Parish." The tree had, in the late nineteenth century, a metal sign nailed to the trunk. This sign, which is now in the collection of the Milton Historical Society, read, "This elm was deeded in 1833 by the First Congregational Church in Milton to Isaac Gulliver who gave a Bond for its perpetual exemption from molestation."

In the early part of the twentieth century, part of the land was used as a pasture for the dairy cows of Thacher Farm. The land, owned by the Sias family, was developed by Richardson. As with all things, Isaac Gulliver's elm eventually began to decay and was allowed to be cut down. The land was developed, with Wendell Park being laid out in 1934 and 1952, Elm Street in 1947 and Gulliver Street in 1941 and 1946. Though the area of the Gulliver Elm and town pound are today covered by one-family residences, the memory of the tree is perpetuated in the names of Gulliver and Elm Streets.

THE RUSSELL HORSE TROUGH

At the triangular junction of Canton Avenue and Centre Street is a large marble and granite horse trough that was given to the Town of Milton in 1909 by Mary H.F. Russell in memory of her husband, Henry Sturgis Russell. Today, a century after it was erected, the fountain is set among dense

The Sturgis Horse Trough was erected in 1909 in memory of Colonel Henry Sturgis Russell (1838–1905). Designed by the Boston architectural firm of Derby & Robinson, it had a "drinking fountain for man and beast…with troughs for horses and dogs." It is at the junction of Canton Avenue and Centre Street and is annually planted by the Milton Garden Club. *Author's collection.*

evergreens and is planted with annuals during the summer months by the Milton Garden Club.

Henry Sturgis Russell (1838–1905) was born at Savin Hill in Dorchester, a fashionable summer resort in the early nineteenth century for Bostonians. His parents, George and Sarah Parkman Shaw Russell, lived on Beacon Hill and were noted for their "great force of character and wide humanity." Educated at Mr. Dixwell's School in Boston and graduated from Harvard College, he was initially employed as a clerk by William Perkins until the advent of the Civil War, when he enlisted in the Union army. Serving from April 1861 to February 1865, he rose to the position of colonel of the Fifth Massachusetts Cavalry. In 1864, the Confederates imprisoned Russell in Libby Prison; following the war, he was brevetted as brigadier general for distinguished conduct during the Battle of Petersburg, Virginia, in June 1864.

In 1863, he had married Mary Hathaway Forbes, daughter of John Murray and Sarah Swain Hathaway Forbes of Milton Hill. The Russells initially lived on Milton Hill but later purchased an extensive tract of land on Canton Avenue opposite Gile Road once being known as Wigwam Hill and now the Indian Cliffs neighborhood. This was to become known as the Home Farm, with both an extensive farm and horse stud on the three-hundred-acre property. Here Russell, said as a child to have "showed a love for horse which amounted almost to a passion," bred Smuggler and Fearnaught, two horses that sired a pedigree line of horses, and maintained the reputation of the well-known Russell Horse Stud.

Though the Russells only lived at Home Farm in the summer, Henry S. Russell was active in the town, serving as assessor, park commissioner and selectman of Milton for six years. Living in Boston's Back Bay in the fashionable Hotel Agassiz on Commonwealth Avenue in the winter, Russell would serve the city of Boston as police commissioner from 1878 to 1880 and fire commissioner from 1895 to 1905. A well-respected and publically minded man, he also served as the president of the Massachusetts Homeopathic Hospital (now part of the Boston University Medical Center) and trustee of the Perkins Institute for the Blind and the Westford Insane Asylum.

Upon his death, his widow "caused to be erected at the junction of Canton Avenue and White Street [now Reedsdale Road], Milton, a beautiful drinking fountain for man and beast, made of fine white granite with troughs for horses and dogs, and it completes one of the prettiest squares of the town and proves a lesson to all passing that way." The fountain was designed by the Boston architectural firm of Derby & Robinson and is five feet high and six feet wide. It has "a large basin for horses, a small drinking place for dogs and bubbling fountains for human beings." The front of the fountain has a carved laurel wreath and garland as its only decoration. With the words "In Memory of Henry Sturgis Russell" carved on the front, it was quietly dedicated on October 5, 1909, when two children unveiled the memorial fountain and the Reverend Roderick Stebbins of the First Parish in Milton spoke briefly for whom it was dedicated and read a poem especially written for the occasion.

THE GREENE HORSE TROUGH

On the triangular lot of land at the intersection of Randolph Avenue and Pleasant Street there is a low granite horse trough that was erected in 1913 in memory of Dr. James Sumner Greene, a resident of the Milton Lower Mills as well as a beloved physician in Milton and Dorchester.

The Greene Horse Trough was erected in memory of Dr. James Sumner Greene (1834–1911) at the junction of Randolph Avenue and Pleasant Street. Designed by Putnam & Allen, the granite fountain and trough was erected to a beloved physician of Milton and Dorchester. It is annually planted by the Milton Amateur Garden Club. *Author's collection.*

James Sumner Greene (1834–1911) was born and raised in Fitchburg, where his father, Solomon Greene, kept a farm. In 1861, he married Laura Tilden of Milton, the daughter of Reverend William Phillips and Mary Foster Tilden who lived on Walnut Street in Milton Centre. She was the sister of the noted architect of the old Milton Town Hall, George T. Tilden, who was in partnership with Henry W. Hartwell in the architectural firm of Hartwell & Tilden from 1877 to 1879 and later with Arthur Rotch in the architectural firm of Rotch & Tilden from 1879 to 1894. At the beginning of the Civil War, in the fall of 1861, James S. Greene was a student at the Harvard Medical School and was appointed by Surgeon General Dale as a hospital steward. He was assigned to the Twenty-first Massachusetts Volunteers, where he was detailed as a medical officer of the Seventh Rhode Island Battery. With this battery, he accompanied General Burnside's expedition to Hatteras Inlet, South Carolina, where he contracted typho-malarial fever. Discharged in the spring of 1862 with this disability, Dr. Greene returned to Boston to complete his medical studies at

Harvard Medical School, which he had entered in 1860, graduating with the degree of doctor of medicine in 1863.

Following his graduation from medical school, the Greenes lived in a comfortable house at 1107 Washington Street, just north of River Street in Milton Lower Mills. With an office on the first floor, he quickly had a flourishing medical practice. He joined the Dorchester Medical Club, the Boston Society for Medical Improvement, the Boston Medical Library Association and the Harvard Medical Alumni Association. A general practitioner for nearly fifty years, he was said to have "a wide acquaintance throughout Dorchester and Milton," and though "delicate in appearance, he was tireless in serving others. His quiet tact and sympathy, and his unfailing kindness endeared him to his patients, who looked to him not only as a skillful physician, but also as a wise counselor and steadfast friend." He was prominent in the Third Religious Society of Dorchester, a Unitarian society founded in 1813 on Richmond Street between Avondale Street and Dorchester Avenue, where he served as senior deacon for many years. Following his death in 1911 from pneumonia, his friends and former patients, headed by Walter Dennison Brooks and Charles D. Rogerson of Milton, raised the funds to erect a memorial fountain through subscription. Successfully petitioned, the Milton granite fountain was designed by Putnam & Allan, a Boston architectural firm headed by Eliot T. Putnam of Milton.

The back of the six-foot-long fountain is composed of blocks of granite, ornamented by two sprays of oak leaves and acorns in honor of Dr. Greene's Scottish ancestry, above which is the inscription "In memory of James Sumner Greene, M.D." and a bronze band of high-relief oak leaves and acorns encircling the fountain's top. There is a granite scroll on either end of the fountain, as well as a trough with two basins and a small bowl carved into the granite top, from which a metal spigot was placed for drinking. Although erected as a horse trough, an arrangement the *Milton Record* said was "highly commended by the S.P.C.A." (Society for the Prevention of Cruelty to Animals), it is today often filled with plants in the summer and evergreen boughs in the winter, thanks to the Milton Amateur Garden Club. It is assumed that as Dr. Greene owned nearly twelve acres of undeveloped land on the east side of Randolph Avenue opposite Highland Street in Milton, the memorial was placed here in 1913 because of its proximity.

The next time you drive past this intersection or stop by Bent's Cookie Factory, slow down and take a look at Dr. Greene's Memorial Fountain. Or better yet, walk over to it and admire Putnam & Allen's elegant design for a "beloved and skillful physician" whose death one hundred years ago was impressively memorialized and fittingly remembered today.

THE TOUZALIN-PIERCE ESTATE

In the post–Civil War era, the daughters of many newly wealthy American families were often encouraged by their parents to seek marriages with aristocratic or, if they were indeed fortunate, royal husbands whose lineage was as sought by the heiresses as their wealth was by their future husbands. Though most of these marriageable maidens lived in New York, one heiress lived in Milton.

Ellen Floyd Touzalin (1872–1950) was the daughter of Albert and Lida Miller Touzalin and lived in Milton in a large Shingle-style house designed by William Ralph Emerson. Her marriage to the Honorable Horace L.A. Hood ended when he was killed during World War I, after which he was knighted posthumously and she was granted the courtesy title Lady Hood of Whitley.

Ellen Floyd Touzalin (1872–1950) was the daughter of Albert and Lida Miller Touzalin, who married in Ohio in 1868. Albert Touzalin (1842–1889) was born in England and immigrated to the United States in 1865, serving as a clerk with the Lake Shore Railroad in Illinois. Over the next two decades, he was associated with the Des Moines Valley, the Burlington & Missouri River, the Atchison, Topeka & Santa Fe and the Chicago, Burlington & Quincy Railroads, increasing in both responsibility and position. In 1868 he married Lida Miller, the daughter of Justice Samuel Freeman Miller of the United States Supreme Court. His sister, Katie Touzalin, also immigrated to this country and married Dr. James Ranson and lived in Burlington, Iowa, a city on the railroad line that her brother was to become associated with. Edward Touzalin was once called "a brilliant man of amazing energy," and his association with Charles Elliott Perkins in the Burlington & Missouri River Railroad (later known as the Chicago, Burlington & Northwest Railroad) led to great personal success and wealth. Eventually, Touzalin became president of the Chicago, Burlington & Northwest Railroad, serving in that capacity until his death.

Touzalin lived in Boston's Back Bay but, in 1885, commissioned Milton architect William Ralph Emerson (1833–1918) to design a large Shingle-style house on a tract of land that he had purchased at Milton Centre. The estate was bounded by Highland Street, Canton Avenue and White Street (now Reeedsdale Road) and could be entered from all three streets. William Ralph Emerson designed numerous houses in Milton, including Three Pines (1876) at 7 Fairfax Street, the Eustis House (1878) at 1426 Canton Avenue, the Barnard-Pierce House (1884) at 289 Adams Street and his own house (1886) at 210 Randolph Avenue. The Touzalin House was similar to these other large houses, but the family only used it in the spring and fall, as their summer house was in Brattleboro, Vermont.

Following the death of Albert Touzalin in 1889, his widow, Lida Miller Touzalin, and daughters Ellen and Charlotte Touzalin moved between their various residences until Ellen F. Touzalin married George Augustus Nickerson (1854–1901) of Boston's Back Bay and Dedham. But she was again left a widow early in her marriage. Mr. Nickerson had been president of the Arlington Mills Corporation in Lawrence and a representative in the state legislature and was said to be at the time of his death Dedham's wealthiest man.

In 1910, Ellen F.T. Nickerson married in Burlington, Iowa, the Honorable Horace Lambert Alexander Hood, KCB, MVO, DSO, younger brother of

The Touzalin-Pierce House was designed by William Ralph Emerson for Albert Touzalin (1842–1890), president of the Chicago, Burlington & Northwest Railroad. Later owned by Wallace Lincoln Pierce (1853–1920), president of S.S. Pierce & Company, and known as Fair Oaks, it was demolished in 1949 to make way for the Milton Hospital, which was designed by Joseph Daniels Leland of the Boston architectural firm of Leland & Larsen. *Author's collection.*

the Fifth Viscount Hood of Whitley. Horace Lambert Hood served as aide-de-camp to King Edward VII in 1912 and was lost in 1916 with HHS *Invincible* in the Battle of Jutland during World War I. He was knighted posthumously by George V, and his widow was granted the courtesy title of Lady Hood, that of a knight's wife. Their son Samuel Hood succeeded his uncle as Sixth Viscount Hood of Whitley, his younger brother Alexander Lambert Hood later succeeding him as the Seventh Viscount Hood of Whitley.

Wallace Lincoln Pierce (1853–1920), president of S.S. Pierce & Company in Boston and son of its founder, Samuel Stillman Pierce, later purchased the Touzalin House, naming it Fair Oaks for the large oak trees on the estate. The Pierce family initially lived here only in the summer, as they kept a town house at 350 Beacon Street in Boston's Back Bay. The house was later lived in by Vassar Pierce (1885–1965), who sold the estate for development as the new site of Milton Hospital, which was designed by Milton architect Joseph Daniels Leland.

The Loew Estate

The Loew Estate off Brush Hill Road was developed from the former Elias M. Loew Estate, which is commemorated by two stone lions guarding the entrance to the property and mature trees that line the new roads. The stone lions surmount a corner of the rubblestone wall, and in the distance are the large houses built a decade ago on Loew Road.

The estate was known as Highfield and was the home of Francis and Rosamond Lawrence Peabody. A member of a prominent family for whom the city of Peabody was named, General Peabody was a graduate of Cheltenham and Trinity Colleges at Cambridge and of the Harvard Law School and was a prominent attorney in Boston, where he was senior partner in the firm of Peabody, Arnold, Batchelder & Luther. He also served as president of the Boston Real Estate Exchange and as judge advocate under Governor William Eustis Russell. Mrs. Peabody was the daughter of Abbott Lawrence, one-time ambassador to the Court of St. James, and sister of Bishop William Lawrence, Episcopal bishop of Massachusetts who kept a house at 1383 Brush Hill Road. The Peabodys, who had lived in Boston's Back Bay and moved in 1896 to Milton full time after General Peabody's unsuccessful mayoral race against Edwin Upton Curtis, built an impressive Colonial Revival house on a ten-acre estate at the crest of Brush Hill. The grounds were landscaped by Rose Standish Nichols, a noted landscape architect whose home has been preserved as the Nichols House Museum on Beacon Hill. The estate included a stable and garage, greenhouses and two teahouses, with impressive terraced gardens. Here they raised their children: Harold (who married Marian Lawrence), Martha (who married Montague W.W. Prowse and lived in Canton on the Peabody stud farm Maresfield), Rosamond (who married B. Nason Hamlin and lived on Brush Hill Road) and Sylvia (who married Clarence V.S. Mitchell).

General Peabody was an avid and successful breeder of racehorses and owned the former stock farm at Ponkapoag known as Maresfield. Here he bred horses that he entered in the Milton horse shows and rode to the Myopia and Norfolk hunts. The stud farm was later inherited by his daughter Martha and her husband, Montague Prowse, and is known today as Prowse Farm. The Peabody heirs sold Highfield to Elias M. Loew in 1940, and he and his flamboyant wife, Sonja Loew, moved from their former home at 1015 Metropolitan Avenue to the estate, where they lived an outré and highly

A stone lion surmounts a rubble stone wall that surrounded Highfield, the Brush Hill Road estate of Francis and Rosamond Lawrence Peabody. In 1940, the estate was purchased by Elias and Sonja Loew (E.M. Loew, the movie mogul) and is today the site of numerous upscale houses on Elias and Loew Roads. *Author's collection.*

ostentatious life. Mr. Loew had opened a string of movie theatres known as E.M. Loew's Theatres throughout the Boston area and had become wealthy through business and real estate ventures. For five decades, the estate deteriorated and, after Mrs. Loew's death (whom E.M. Loew had divorced many years before but continued to live in a wing of the mansion), was eventually demolished. Elias and Loew Roads were laid out and the former estate was subdivided for large houses, which are still guarded by the stone lions that in their sphinx-like pose flank the entrance from Brush Hill Road.

East Milton Square

In this photograph, the intersection of Adams and Willard Streets and Granite and Bryant Avenues is a bustling scene about 1915. With automobiles, horse-drawn wagons and electric streetcars, East Milton Square was a major crossroads a century ago.

From the left can be seen the Merrill Building, then occupied by Hodges Drug Store, which still stands and is now known as the Rugby Building with

East Milton Square was developed as "Railway Village" after the granite industry started in 1826. Street traffic, including horse-drawn wagons, automobiles and a streetcar from Quincy, created a bustling intersection in 1905. On the right is the Ellsworth Building, which is now the site of the Milton Post Office, and the Hose No. 2 Engine House is in the center.

Cee Jay's Sandwich Shop on the first floor; next is the hose house of the Milton Fire Department, a wood building that was replaced by the present red brick East Milton Fire House, which was occupied in 1953. In front of the hose house can be seen the Thayer Fountain, the gift in 1911 to the town from Nathaniel Thayer Kidder (1860–1938), a noted philanthropist and the first Milton tree warden. Designed by Ludvig S. Ipsen, the fountain was of Westerly granite and was described in the newspaper as a "broad trough for horses on the street side of the fountain and on the other side a bubbling fountain for human beings and at the bottom a little trough for dogs." This artistic fountain had three frolicking dolphins carved in granite above the horse trough and is, since its removal in the mid-1950s, a notable loss to the square. The horse trough portion of the fountain was salvaged and was later placed by the town at Algerine Corner, the junction of Adams, Pleasant and Centre Streets, where it still remains.

Ludvig Sandoe Ipsen (1840–1920) was sketched in 1904 by his artist son, Ernest L. Ipsen. Ipsen was a noted architect, designer and book plate artist, and he designed the Kidder Fountain, donated to the town by Nathaniel Thayer Kidder, ensuring a "bubbling fountain for human beings and at the bottom a little trough for dogs." *Author's collection.*

On Willard Street (now Granite Avenue), to the right of the hose house, are the Sweeney and Barry Houses and the stable of McGuire & O'Hearn Granite Works, all of which are now used for commercial enterprises. On the right is the Ellsworth Building, an impressive Colonial Revival wood commercial block that stood where the Southeast Expressway now passes through the square. On the first floor of this block, which was owned by Henry E. Sheldon, were the Charles Mullen Meat & Provisions, the Charles E. Snow (later McDonald's) Dry Goods Store and the J.J. Hammers Pharmacy. Notice the mortar and pestle (the sign of a druggist) in front of Hammers's store, set on a square column, just below the sign advertising "Drugs."

The electric streetcars seen in the center of the photograph on Granite Avenue connected Milton to Quincy and Braintree and are stopped at the intersection; the Quincy Branch of the Old Colony Railroad passed through the square, running parallel with Granite Avenue. Originally the path of the Granite Railway, laid out in 1826 by Gridley Bryant (1789–1867)—for whom Bryant Avenue was named—it later became, after 1890, a major commuter station that was located on the immediate left for those traveling to Boston for business or pleasure. Unfortunately, the Old Colony Railroad was discontinued in Milton in 1940 due to a lack of ridership. Today, though Hodge's Drug Store (the Rugby Building) still exists at 537 Adams Street with its interesting façade and projecting marquee, East Milton Square is drastically different. These changes began in 1953, when a town hearing was held in Milton on the proposed Southeast Expressway, and 1954, when the work on excavating the square actually began. In 1955, the underpass was named for Josiah Babcock Jr., and in 1957, the new roadway was opened for traffic. Over four decades later, the overpass at East Milton was redesigned and laid out for public use as a community park. It was dedicated in 1997 in honor of M. Joseph Manning, a longtime representative to the Massachusetts House. In reflecting on the photograph, one can readily see the dramatic changes in East Milton in the twentieth century and wonder what's next for East Milton.

East Milton

In the accompanying photograph, Squantum Street in East Milton can be seen with a couple in a horse-drawn carriage crossing the railroad tracks of the Old Colony Railroad, with a railroad crossing guard peering from the pyramidal-roofed guard box on the right. Cary Hill can be seen in the distance. It's obvious from the open, rolling fields that Milton had extensive tracts of undeveloped land at the turn of the twentieth century that would be laid out for residential areas following World War II.

The Old Colony Railroad, which followed the original route of the Granite Railway that was laid out in 1826 from Quincy to the Neponset River, connected Boston and South Shore towns. This spur had a railroad depot in East Milton and continued on to Quincy. This route later became known as the Granite Branch of the New York, New Haven and Hartford Railroad. It is interesting to note that there is a wood sign above the crossing that states "Railroad Crossing—Look Out—Engine," which, hopefully, if one didn't hear the great steam engine approaching, would alert you to at least be cautious. The small Greek Revival cottage just past the railroad crossing belonged to the Fenno family (moved in the mid-1950s to the corner of Canton Avenue and Hemlock Street) and has an interesting grouping of outbuildings that connote the farm aspect of the area.

Squantum Street in East Milton connected Adams Street and Granite Avenue, and the Granite Branch of the Old Colony Railroad can be seen in the foreground. The Cary Estate can be seen on the left and Eastover, the Bowditch Estate, on the far right.

East Milton Square, the junction of Adams Street and Granite Avenue, was a busy crossroads as seen from the roof of the East Milton Firehouse in 1950. In 1955, the area was excavated for the Southeast Expressway (Route 93), a suppressed six-lane highway with an overpass at Adams Street named for Representative Josiah Babcock Jr. Today, the overpass has become a community park named in honor of M. Joseph Manning, a longtime representative.

In the distance, on the left can be seen the Italianate house of Edward Cary (1828–1888) and Alice Hathaway Forbes Cary, who owned an extensive tract of land that is today bisected by Cary Avenue and Cabot Road; on the far right can be seen Eastover, the estate of Ernest and Margaret Swann Bowditch, now 366 Adams Street. Named for the fact that the estate overlooked East Milton ("over" East Milton), it was indicative, with the Cary House, of the large estates that spanned Adams Street in the nineteenth and early twentieth centuries. The open land, which is today bisected by Pillon, Taff, Augusta, Hurlcroft and Christopher Roads, had been hayed in the late fall, as the ribbing that is accentuated by the snow cover shows the tractor's neat rows.

Today, this area of Squantum Street in East Milton passes over the Southeast Expressway, a multilane highway that cut a wide swath through the town in the late 1950s. The area seen in the photograph has changed drastically, with numerous houses having been built on newly laid out streets between 1930 and 1960, when the railroad service was discontinued over forty years ago.

KERRIGAN'S CORNER

In the accompanying photograph, the intersection of Brook Road and White Street (now known as Reedsdale Road) and Central Avenue is seen in the early twentieth century from the roof of Milton High School. Unofficially named for Bernard J. Kerrigan, the intersection is today built up with numerous houses and a brick professional building.

Bernard J. Kerrigan (1850–1914) was a native of County Leitrim, Ireland. He immigrated to the United States and initially lived in the Atlantic section of Quincy until 1887, when he moved to Milton, living in the center of town for the next twenty-seven years. Kerrigan was employed at O.S. Godfrey & Company in Milton Village for over twenty years. Otis S. Godfrey had opened a coal business in 1865, supplying Milton with anthracite coal that was brought to Milton Village by coastal schooners. The coal was then delivered by horse teams, and Bernard Kerrigan operated one of the forty horse teams; he later was employed by the Town of Milton in the Street Department for the last two years of his life. Not famous in the traditional sense of noted Milton residents, he was well respected in town.

Kerrigan's Corner is the junction of Reedsdale Road, Central Avenue and Brook Road. The corner was named for Bernard Kerrigan (1850–1914,) a well-respected town employee and father of John F. Kerrigan, whose grocery store was once a popular place for students at the high school. A Wason G-bench open streetcar on Brook Road approaches Kerrigan's Corner around 1900.

The accompanying photograph shows a Wason 1 G-bench open streetcar on Brook Road approaching Kerrigan's Corner sometime after 1909. The streetcar lines came late to Milton; the line began in 1899, and the electric streetcars traveled along Brook Road, Central Avenue, White Street (Reedsdale Road), Pleasant Street and Edge Hill Road and connected the town to other lines in Boston and Quincy. It has been said that the "introduction of the street railway caused a revolution in transportation nearly as great as that later brought by the automobile." On the far left can be seen the corner of the estate of James Savage Russell and Turner's Pond on the upper left, which was owned by J. Arthur Turner, then an ice pond for cutting ice that was used in iceboxes, which were the predecessor of our refrigerator. The bottom center of the photograph shows the open land of the Tilden family on either side of Central Avenue, and on the far right is White Street (Reedsdale Road). On the opposite side of the street is the one-story general store of John Kerrigan and, on the left, the house of Patrick

J.F. Kerrigan's store was at the corner of Brook Road and Central Avenue, where one was encouraged to drink Milton Spring Ginger Ale and enjoy Rose's ice cream. John F. Kerrigan offered cigars, confections, soda drinks, ice cream and a wide range of necessary items, as well as a place for socialization for many years. *Courtesy of Bernadette C. Richards.*

Cunningham. Today, a brick professional building is located at 2 Reedsdale Road, which was originally a general store, ice cream parlor and gas line pumps owned by John F. Kerrigan, the son of Bernard Kerrigan.

The store that preceded it is shown in the photo at the junction of Brook Road and Central Avenue. It was replaced as the business grew, and the building was remodeled in 1955 as a pharmacy and operated first by Joseph and Leonard Mindel and then by Daniel Wein and later the Palumbo family (notice the mortar and pestle painted on the glass of the cupola). Dr. Richard Delany later remodeled the building as his medical office in the 1970s. John and James Kerrigan lived in a duplex house at 493–495 Central Avenue, near the corner of Thacher Street, where the Kerrigan and Naughton families had lived for many years.

Though Milton High School is today located at the comer of Central Avenue and Brook Road, the school building was originally built as the Vose School. Old Milton High School, which was designed by Milton architect Bradford O. Hamilton, was built in 1885 and stood on Engine Street beside the Central Firehouse; on the opposite side of the street was the Thatcher School, which was built on the present site of the Council on Aging. When the Vose and High School buildings were swapped in 1911, the Vose School (the former high school) was used until it was demolished in 1956. The high school (the former Vose School) was until recently in use but with additions of a science wing, gymnasium, assembly hall and locker rooms. Though unofficially called "Kerrigan's Corner" for most of the twentieth century, it might now be appropriate for the town to officially mark the intersection in memory of Bernard and John Kerrigan.

Chapter 8

FELLOW MILTONIANS

THOMAS HUTCHINSON

Thomas Hutchinson, the last royal governor of Massachusetts Bay Colony, was said by John Adams, second president of the United States, to have "been admired, revered, rewarded, and almost adored; and the idea was common that he was the greatest and best man in America." Unfortunately, he was a Loyalist and left Milton in 1774 for a life of exile in London due to his unswerving beliefs.

Thomas Hutchinson (1711–1780) was born and raised in Boston's North End, though his ancestor William Hutchinson (1586–1642) had owned property in Milton in the seventeenth century. Educated at the North Grammar School and graduated in 1727 from Harvard College, he began his career in his father's counting house in Boston, where it was said that "he was shrewd and energetic." Becoming a successful merchant, he was elected as a representative to the General Court in 1737 and was made a selectman of Boston at the same time. His talents were soon recognized, and he was chosen a member of the council and "became one of the most popular men in the colony." He was joined in marriage in 1734 to Margaret Sanford, granddaughter of Governor Sanford of Rhode Island, and they lived in great splendor in a brick mansion on Half Moon Street in Boston's North End. After 1743, they also kept a countryseat, known as Unquety, on Milton Hill; he once described this as "the place [he] loved best."

Thomas Hutchinson (1711–1780) was the last royal governor of Massachusetts Bay Colony. A man considered to be "admired, revered, rewarded, and almost adored" during his lifetime, he was a Loyalist who departed Milton in 1774 to report to King George III of the tumultuous times in Boston. He would spend the remainder of his life as an exile in London due to his unswerving beliefs.

Hutchinson was once described as a "man of good character, of unwearyingly industry and high intellectual attainments," and was well respected; he was appointed lieutenant governor of Massachusetts in 1756 and chief justice in 1760. As a representative of King George III, Hutchinson had political clout, but he was to encounter tremendous opposition by his fellow colonists when he accused certain Boston merchants of smuggling and evading the taxes imposed by the King on trade in the colonies. This action was well warranted but proved so unpopular that Hutchinson was vilified by the mob, and Andrew Oliver, his brother-in-law, resigned his post as distributor of the hated tax stamps. So detested had Hutchinson become that his mansion was mobbed in 1765 by "the most thoroughly organized rabble" in Boston, under the instigation of Sam Adams and William Cooper of the Caucus Club, and was completely destroyed. This was not just retaliation against him for supposedly having an inordinate lust for power, but rather that his staunchest enemies "feared his eloquence, his attractive presence, his learning and his honored name," and he thereby sealed his fate. The Hutchinson family left Boston and made their home at Unquety after 1765, with the governor traveling to Boston by his phaeton or by barge from the Milton town landing. Milton was less affected by the turmoil in Boston; however, in 1770, the Boston Massacre brought the smoldering situation to the forefront, and Hutchinson and his fellow commissioners were in direct conflict with the people, who were in dispute with the assembly and council.

Unquety was the countryseat of Governor Thomas Hutchinson and was the described as "the place [he] loved best." Built in 1764, it stood at the corner of Adams and Hutchinson Streets on Milton Hill. Demolished in 1871 by the Russell family, a large Victorian mansion was built on the foundations, and that house was used as the headquarters of the local Red Cross during World War II.

So serious had the political situation become that in 1773 Hutchinson sent "a message to the Assembly in which he asserted the supreme authority of Parliament" and thereby provoked even more acrimonious discussions between the people who came to be identified as the Sons of Liberty. In 1774, just down the hill from Hutchinson's countryseat, a group of representatives signed the Suffolk Resolves, which had been drawn up as a list of nineteen grievances against the impositions of Hutchinson's rulings and the severe measures imposed on the colony by the King and Parliament. In so untenable a position was he placed that Hutchinson left Milton, a place where he was "universally respected and beloved by neighbors and townsmen," in 1774 to report the situation directly to George III. Though he was "graciously received by the king and offered a baronetcy," he refused the honor due to a lack of funds. Hutchinson had left the New World with little, leaving his estate in Milton and numerous properties in and around Boston to be confiscated by the new government. He lived the remainder of his life as an exile in Brompton, a suburb near London. After the confiscation of his property, Hutchinson's estate in Milton was sold to Samuel Broome and later to James and Mercy Otis Warren; the property was later purchased in 1812 by Barney Smith, who lived there in great style, which was continued by his descendants, the Russells. Today, the governor's estate on Milton Hill is remembered by Hutchinson Street, which was laid through the property in the nineteenth century.

Thomas Hutchinson is an enigma, for it was "his lot to live in a period when the loyalty to royal authority, which had been a main part of his education and his life thought, was suddenly brought into conflict with revolutionary ideas and aspirations." In the same circumstances, who of us would fail to do what was considered the right thing? "The man who had been a sworn officer of the king for twenty-five years could scarcely be expected to change the habit of a lifetime and revoke his allegiance."

ASAPH CHURCHILL

Asaph Churchill was a noted attorney and leading citizen of Milton in the early nineteenth century. As an elderly gentleman, he was well respected by his fellow townsmen for his ability as an attorney as well as his benevolence and generosity to the less fortunate.

Mr. Churchill (1765–1841) was born in Middleboro, Massachusetts, and according to his genealogical entry in the book *The Churchills in America*, he worked in an iron foundry as a young boy. Though he worked in this menial job, he was tutored in Latin and Greek in his youth and fitted for college. According to family tradition, he departed Middleboro in 1785, taking "his little bundle of earthly belongings, including his only pair of shoes," and walked barefoot to Harvard College, where he sat for and passed the entrance exam. Following his graduation, in the class of 1789, he studied law with John Davis, Esq., and was admitted to the Plymouth County Bar in 1793. After establishing a successful law practice and perceived by the public to be "one of the ablest lawyers in Norfolk County," he settled in Milton in 1810 after purchasing the former home of Lieutenant Governor Edward Hutchinson Robbins (1758–1829) at the corner of Adams Street and Back Lane, originally laid out in 1661 and known as Middle Street by 1825, and eventually to be known as Churchills Lane. The house, which still stands at 233 Adams Street, was built in 1740 by Colonel Joseph Gooch (1700–1770) and is similar in its architectural style to the Suffolk Resolves House.

In Milton, Mr. Churchill became an active citizen, representing the town in the legislature in 1810 and 1812. He was said to be "a man of public spirit and enterprise, but of independent disposition and strong individuality," which, in my opinion, meant that he was a thoroughly cantankerous character! In 1810, the year he purchased the old Gooch-Robbins House, he married Mary Gardner, the daughter of Dr. Edward Gardner of Charlestown; Mrs. Churchill was said to be a "lady of distinguished beauty and lovely character," but she also must have been a great diplomat to be married to a man of such "independent disposition."

Asaph Churchill briefly served in the War of 1812 but soon returned to Milton, where he had extensive landholdings throughout the town and in Dorchester. The Churchills were the parents of seven children, among them Asaph Churchill, who married Mary Buckminster Brewer and later Mary Ann Ware, who in 1891 built 97 Randolph Avenue on land subdivided from his father's vast landholdings in Milton. His grandson, Asaph Churchill, built 247 Adams Street.

SIMON WILLARD

Simon Willard is considered one of the finest clockmakers in American history. His tall clocks were made by hand and placed in impressive "Roxbury cases," and he also made patent timepieces, commonly known as banjo clocks, which were prized possessions when new and today are coveted by families who inherited them as well as by collectors alike.

Simon Willard (1753–1848) was the seventh son of Benjamin and Sarah Brooks Willard and was raised on a farm in Grafton, where he and three of his brothers—Benjamin, Aaron and Ephraim—became clockmakers. Simon was apprenticed at the age of thirteen to Mr. Morris in Grafton, learning his trade as a clockmaker. During the Revolution, he served in the Grafton Militia Company under Captain Aaron Kimball and was a

Simon Willard (1753–1848) is considered one of the finest clockmakers in American history. He patented the banjo clock and produced impressive Roxbury tall case clocks at his shop "At the Sign of the New Clock" in Roxbury. They were as prized then as they are now. He lived with his daughter, Mary Willard Hobart, on Ruggles Lane in Milton. *Author's collection.*

Minuteman who responded to the Lexington alarm. In 1775, he married Hannah Willard, his first cousin, who died in childbirth the next year; his second wife was Mary Bird Leeds (1763–1823), the daughter of Edward and Mary Starr Bird of Dorchester and the widow of Richard Leeds, by whom he had eleven children.

Willard, along with his brother Aaron, moved to Roxbury in 1780, to a small wood-framed house at 2196 Roxbury (now Washington) Street, which led to "the Neck," the only land route into Boston and a prime location for his business. He lived and worked "At the Sign of the New Clock," a large clock that projected from the building and became a prominent landmark. His "habits of industry, and the intense study of his art, left him but little time for attention to matters of public interest." As a clockmaker and an ingenious inventor, he patented in 1784 a clock jack that was used for roasting meat by rotation. In 1802, his "Willard Patent Timepiece" was recorded, and in 1819 his patent for an alarm clock was recorded; he also invented the machinery for the revolving lights for lighthouses. However, his skill as a hand maker of clocks was unrivaled and led to his being appointed, for fifty years, as keeper of the clocks at Harvard College and commissions for a clock in the United States Capitol and the University of Virginia, as well as gallery clocks (Roxbury Meetinghouse and the Second Church in Dorchester) and numerous turret clocks throughout New England. He retired in 1839 after seven decades of success with a name that had become synonymous with high-quality timepieces. He "passed his time in his family and shop; for the enjoyment of which 'age withered not his powers.'"

In later life, following the death of his wife in 1823, Simon Willard lived successively with his children, first at the home of Simon Willard Jr. in Boston, then with Edward and Sarah Brooks Willard Bird on Boston Street (now Columbia Road) adjacent to the Old North Burying Ground and later with his daughter Mary, the wife of Caleb Hobart. The Hobarts lived in an old house, later known as the Ruggles House, near the corner of Canton Avenue and Ruggles Lane in Milton, and here Caleb Hobart (1768–1843) worked as a butcher dealing chiefly in mutton. Hobart, a very married man, having two wives and a large family before he married Mary Willard, owned a large tract of land just west of his home that was referred to as Golgotha, as "it was used as a place to dispose of the refuse from his slaughter house." Of course, in the Bible Jesus was crucified at Mount Calvary, and Golgotha was known as the "place of the skull." However, this area of Columbine and Valley Roads in the elegant Columbines, where Hobart deposited the accumulated refuse of his slaughterhouse, was so called for the vast amount of bones dumped there.

In the mid-1840s, Mary Willard Hobart (1793–1855) took her father in to live with her, as she had become a widow in 1843. Simon Willard, then an elderly man, had unimpaired sight and hearing and was described by his grandson Alexander Claxton Cary as being a "little figure sitting in his arm chair by the window in Aunt Mary's room at Milton. He used to sit in this arm chair most all day, now and then taking a short pair of steps by which he could reach the clock in the room, and opening it would do some little thing to it probably from habit, rather than from any fixing the clock needed. This clock was one of his own Timepieces…My brother tells me that at Milton, Grandfather went to visit Gen. [Moses] Whitney one day, upon coming home, our man Elijah offered to help Grandfather out of team. 'Don't help me out, don't help me out,' said Grandfather 'they will think I am an old man.'"

Indeed, by the mid-1840s, Simon Willard was an old man, a grand old man, and had a justifiable reputation that was hard to emulate, even by his successful apprentices and rivals. He died in 1848 at the home of Isaac and Julia Willard Cary in Boston and was buried in the Eustis Street Burial Ground in Roxbury. His daughter Mary Hobart later moved her parents' remains to her lot at Forest Hills Cemetery, where a Gothic brownstone monument designed by Alpheus Cary marks his final resting place. As it said in his obituary in the *Boston Daily Advertiser*, "Mr. Willard, after his long dealings with Time, has now left him for eternity. Pease [*sic*] to his blameless and honest memory!"

BENJAMIN SMITH ROTCH

Benjamin Smith Rotch was a Boston merchant who kept a farm known as Pine Tree Brook in Milton in the nineteenth century and once owned over one hundred acres on both sides of the Blue Hills Parkway, originally known as Mattapan Street, including the present site of HOME, Inc. Benjamin Smith Rotch (1817–1882) was descended from the prominent whale ship owner William Rotch of New Bedford, who was "the first to establish our whale fisheries in Europe" and thereby increase his wealth and prominence.

A graduate of Harvard College, it was said of Benjamin Rotch that from "the beginning he lived up to the family traditions, and his whole life was the embodiment of the finer elements of the race to which he belonged."

Starting his career as a merchant in New Bedford, he soon became involved in manufacturing, founding with his brother William Morgan Rotch the New Bedford Cordage Company. Their business sense served them well, and the Rotches soon became prominent in manufacturing in New Bedford. Mr. Rotch married Annie Lawrence in 1846; she was the daughter of the wealthy manufacturer for whom Lawrence, Massachusetts, was named, and the Rotches lived at 3 Commonwealth Avenue beside the town house of Abbott Lawrence in Boston's Back Bay. During trips abroad, the young couple was able to improve and cultivate their interest in art and architecture. "Gifted with a refined taste and sensitive feeling for form and

Pine Tree Brook was the one-hundred-acre farm of Benjamin Smith Rotch (1817–1882) at the corner of Mattapan Street (now Blue Hills Parkway) and Canton Avenue. Here Rotch raised Alderny and Jersey cattle and had a dairy named for the estate. In the 1970s, Aimee and Rosamond Lamb, granddaughters of Rotch, sold the estate to the town, and it was developed as HOME Inc. *Courtesy of the Boston Athenaeum.*

color, his careful study of foreign collections...made him a competent and fastidious critic, as well as a painter, whose landscapes have been shown to advantage." His pastoral estate in Milton, which was entered by now damaged un-capped stone piers that remain on the Blue Hills Parkway to the left of the entrance to Pine Tree Brook, might have offered him fodder for personal painting, but he was unselfish in this regard and often assisted artists with "the timely help which was so unostentatiously and freely given."

The Rotch Farm in Milton had extensive lands that were cultivated with both crops and fruit trees and also provided grazing room for a herd of Jersey and Alderney cattle. With Thomas Motley, whose farm in Jamaica Plain was known as Forest Hills, Mr. Rotch was the first to import to the United States these two new strains of cattle. The aspect of stock breeding cattle had become more pronounced in the early decades of the nineteenth century, with the goal to breed a new strain of cattle that would surpass the old. With Mr. Motley, who served as an officer of the Massachusetts Society for the Promotion of Agriculture, Mr. Rotch financed these stock breeding experiments, which were exhibited at the Brighton Cattle Show, where they "had stimulated a spirit of emulation, engendered a dramatic improvement in the quality of Massachusetts livestock, and spread knowledge and appreciation of agriculture." However, Mr. Rotch was also interested in architecture, and his eldest son, Arthur Rotch, was educated as an architect at both the Massachusetts Institute of Technology and L'Ecole des Beaux-Arts in Paris.

Upon his untimely death, Mr. Rotch's family carried out his intentions to establish a scholarship for architects to travel abroad and thereby encourage the art. In 1883, his children founded the Rotch Traveling Scholarship as a memorial to him, and it has been given annually to an aspiring Massachusetts architect as "an incentive to earnest study which will yearly profit more than the one who wins the prize." As a tribute to this man whose "good judgment always made him a wise councilor," his family also decided to build the Church of the Holy Spirit at Mattapan in his memory. Designed in 1886 by his son Arthur Rotch, partner of George T. Tilden in the firm of Rotch & Tilden, the church was commissioned by Annie Rotch Lamb, wife of Horatio A. Lamb, who later was to inherit the farm in Milton. A country church built of Roxbury puddingstone, it has a squat tower in the center with Tudor-inspired gables projecting from it. The church, consecrated by Bishop Phillips Brooks, was furnished with gifts from the family, including

Rosamond Lamb (1898–1989) was painted by her artist sister, Aimee Lamb (1893–1989). The Lamb sisters used the Milton estate in spring and fall but lived in Boston's Back Bay and summered on an island off Bar Harbor, Maine. Aimee Lamb was a noted artist, having studied at the Museum of Fine Arts. The Lamb sisters, upon their deaths, bequeathed their fortune to numerous charities. *Author's collection.*

the organ, silver communion service, pulpit and altar. The church was set in landscaped grounds at the comer of River Street and Cummins Highway, then a far more rural area than it has become today.

Today, the Church of the Holy Spirit remains as a memorial to Benjamin Smith Rotch, but his farm in Milton was sold by his granddaughters Aimee and Rosamond Lamb for development by HOME, Inc. as Pine Tree Brook, an elegant senior housing community. Though his house is gone, the stone piers on the Blue Hills Parkway recall the old Rotch Farm and the Jersey and Alderney cattle that were once bred in Milton.

HENRY A. WHITNEY

Henry Austin Whitney (1826–1883) was a successful nineteenth-century businessman, serving as president of the Boston and Providence Railroad. A summer resident of Milton, his estate was on the western corner of Blue Hill Avenue and Robbins Street, now part of Delphi Academy and numerous private homes.

The son of Joseph and Elizabeth Pratt Whitney, Henry A. Whitney was born on Purchase Street in Boston and was a constant visitor to Harris's Folly, his grandfather's house, which was a large house at the corner of High and Pearl Streets in Boston's old colonial South End. Joseph Whitney and Henderson Inches shared the impressive brick house as a grand duplex in what was then a fashionable neighborhood of Boston. Educated at a boarding school on Cape Cod and later at the Chauncey Hall School in Boston, Henry Whitney graduated from Harvard College in 1846, serving as marshal of his class. A great favorite of both his fellow classmates and faculty at college, Mr. Whitney was described long after his graduation by a

Henry Austin Whitney (1826–1883) was the president of the Boston and Providence Railroad. Once described as having a "high sense of honor…a truly good heart," he was a successful businessman as well as admired in every circle in Boston and Milton. *Courtesy of Rosamond Whitney Carr.*

fellow classmate as being "so kind and affectionate to all his classmates, and was so much the channel through which we communicated with the College and with each other, that it seems as if the whole class were dead" following his own death in 1883.

Entering his father's business following his graduation from college, Mr. Whitney was to become a leading merchant in Boston. During his long and successful business career, he was to serve as a director of the Merchants and Miners' Transportation Company, president of the Suffolk National Bank from 1874 to 1876 and president of the Boston and Providence Railroad from 1874 to 1883. A benevolent and concerned citizen of Boston, where he spent his winters, and Milton, where he spent his summers, Mr. Whitney's "stern integrity and high sense of honor made themselves felt, and inspired confidence, his kindly and genial manner, not at all artificial, but springing from a truly good heart, conciliated the regard alike of friend and stranger."

Mr. Whitney married Fanny Lawrence, the daughter of Boston merchant William Lawrence, in 1852; she was described as "a most affectionate and devoted wife…[and] his constant companion both at home and on all his journeys, whether of business or pleasure." They were the parents of Henry Lawrence Whitney, Joseph Cutler Whitney, Ellerton Pratt Whitney, Elizabeth Whitney Minot, Constance Whitney Zerrahn and Hugh Whitney. An educated and erudite gentleman, Mr. Whitney amassed a fine research library "of about five thousand volumes, rich especially in editions of Milton, in books relating to Milton, and to early Massachusetts and New England history. He did a good deal in the way of genealogical research, but wrote little for publication except occasional articles on passing events, biographical notices of friends and classmates, and pamphlets in regard to mercantile affairs." Interested in history, he was a member of the prestigious Massachusetts Historical Society, the oldest of its kind in this country, and of the New England Historic and Genealogical Society. He displayed a great interest in the publication of Reverend Albert Teele's *History of Milton*, "toward which he contributed a sum of money sufficient to defray the cost of the woodcuts of the old houses of the town, which, but for his liberality, it would have lacked."

The Whitney Estate had as its seat "an artistic modern structure [that] presents a striking contrast among the building of olden times," as seen in the accompanying photograph from one of his descendants. A massive

The Whitney Mansion was a large, rambling Victorian mansion that surmounted the crest at the corner of Blue Hill Avenue and Robbins Street. Said to be "an artistic modern [1875] structure [that] presents a striking contrast among the building of olden times," it had massive roofs and gables with soaring chimneys, banks of windows, mock Tudor detailing, heavily bracketed overhangs and an impressive glass veranda. *Courtesy of Henry Carr.*

Victorian mansion of red brick and brownstone with a slate roof punctuated by soaring chimneys, it was built circa 1875 on the ridge just south of Blue Hill Avenue between Robbins Street and Barbara Lane overlooking rolling lawns that extended to Canton Avenue and into the meadows and forest beyond. The house was approached through gates on Blue Hill Avenue.

A cottage still standing at 562 Blue Hill Avenue (now a part of Delphi Academy) is all that remains. The house, with banks of windows, mock Tudor detailing on the gables and heavily bracketed overhangs, had an impressive glass veranda, seen on the right, that was bathed in sunlight every afternoon from the south and west. Following the deaths of Henry and Fanny Whitney, the house was inherited by Ellerton Pratt and Ellen Cushman Sargeant Whitney. A portion of the estate was subdivided, and Overlook was built by Franz and Constance Whitney Zerrahn at 152 Robbins Street, later to be owned by Sarah and Mary Andrews and later Nelson Curtis Jr.

Though the Whitney Mansion was unfortunately razed about 1940 following a fire, the estate would later see the McGinley House (designed by Bigelow and Wadsworth and built at 582 Blue Hill Avenue) and the Donald House (designed by Joseph Leland and built at 638 Blue Hill Avenue) and, following World War II, the land being further subdivided for new houses on the newly cut-through streets Alfred Road, Barbara Lane and Meetinghouse Lane. Although a small wood-framed cottage is all that survives of this once impressive estate, Henry Austin Whitney was a well-known merchant and railroad entrepreneur in the nineteenth century and an important part of the success of Teele's *History of Milton*.

EMILY FIFIELD

There is an elementary school on Dunbar Avenue in Dorchester that was named for Emily Fifield, a noted educator, advocate for manual training in the public schools and the second female member of the Boston School Committee. A resident of Morton Road in Milton, she was well known for her work in the Woman's Alliance of the Unitarian Church, of which she served as national recording secretary for three decades.

Emily Porter Fifield (1840–1913) was born in Weymouth, the daughter of Thomas Brastow and Emily Vining Porter. Married in 1858 to Dr. William Cranch Bond Fifield, she lived in Harrison Square, a neighborhood in Dorchester now referred to as "Clam Point," for five decades. The Fifields purchased a ready-built house from John Robinson on Ashland Street, which had been developed following the opening of the Old Colony Railroad. As a teacher in the Sunday school of the First Parish in Dorchester, she was to be elected to the Boston School Committee in 1884 as the second woman ever elected to that position; her predecessor was Abby May, an early exponent of the equal suffrage movement, whose sister was Mary May White Boardman of Brush Hill Road in Milton. These two women were shortly joined by Mary P.T. Hemenway, a wealthy philanthropist and founder of the manual arts and domestic science classes in the Boston Public Schools, whose summer house was on Canton Avenue. The introduction of sewing and cooking for girls and woodworking, sloyd and manual arts for boys prepared them for a job following their education, for far fewer went on to college a century ago. A respected authority on public school matters, Mrs. Fifield had nationwide

Emily Porter Fifield, *left,* and her daughter, Mary Fifield King, sit in the garden of Kingfield at 77 Morton Road in Milton. Mrs. Fifield was the second female member of Boston School Committee and was an advocate for manual training and educational matters, traveling nationwide to lecture on the topics. Her daughter was a local antiquarian and historian of the First Parish Church in Dorchester. *Author's collection.*

fame as an advocate of manual training. It was said of her that she "traveled widely, lecturing on manual training and educational matters, and was a prominent advocate of the more extended use of the city's school plant."

Mrs. Fifield "adopted" the Mechanic Arts School (later known as Boston Technical High School) and chaired a subcommittee on that school that was "largely instrumental in causing its marked success." At that time, Mechanic Arts was a major feeder of students to "Tech," as the Massachusetts Institute of Technology was known. Upon her husband's death in 1896, Mrs. Fifield donated the funds and furnishings for the Fifield Room in the Boston Medical Library in his memory and thereafter began to retire from her numerous committees.

She would later move to Morton Hill in Milton in 1911, having the noted architect Edwin J. Lewis Jr. (1859–1937) design her house at 77

Morton Road on land she had purchased from Nathaniel Safford. Mr. Lewis, a fellow member of the First Parish in Dorchester, had designed a Shingle-style house with bold Tuscan columns on the front and side porches. Mrs. Fifield and her daughter and son-in-law, Mary Fifield and Henry King, moved into the house in 1911, laying out perennial gardens that were planted with cuttings and roots from friends' gardens. The Fifield-King House was to become known as Kingfield after 1913 in honor of Henry King's surname and the "field" of Fifield. Mr. Lewis was to design five houses in Milton: two for Ridgeway Holbrook (331 Randolph Avenue and 45 Westside Road), the Fifield House (77 Morton Road), the Hayward House (86 Morton Road) and the Brooks House (87 Morton Road). Mr. Lewis was educated at the School of Architecture at MIT and was associated with Peabody & Stearns from 1881 to 1887, when he began a private architectural practice that would extend for the next five decades.

Upon her death at Kingfield in 1913, Mrs. Fifield was eulogized as a generous, concerned citizen whose efforts for the Mariners' House in Boston's North End, the School for the Feeble Minded Youth in South Boston and the Independent Voters' League did not go unnoticed.

MABEL HUNT SLATER

The Slater Mill in Pawtucket, Rhode Island, is the oldest manufacturer of textiles in this country. The mill was founded in 1790 by Samuel Slater, a recent immigrant from Britain, under the name Almy, Brown & Slater and is today the site of a museum that honors not only the man but also the industry that revolutionized the aspect of cotton textile weaving in this country.

Samuel Slater (1768–1835) was apprenticed in England as a weaver to Richard Arkwright and Jedidiah Strutt, whose inventions revolutionized cotton spinning. As a trained artisan, he was barred from leaving Britain, should he possibly expose trade secrets, as it was thought that the United States offered a greater field for the textile industry than Britain could afford. Leaving England with no models, plans or detailed drawings, Slater arrived in Pawtucket, Rhode Island, in 1790, where he constructed and erected, remarkably from memory, textile machinery that produced yarn equal to the quality of that spun in Britain and commenced the first commercially

Pine Bank was designed by Paul Hunt for his sister Mabel Hunt Slater as her "in between house," as she kept a Back Bay town house and a summer house in Maine. Jeanne d'Arc Academy later purchased the estate and operated a day and boarding school; today, this is part of the campus of Curry College. *Author's collection.*

successful textile mill in the United States. His business was to become the model for his successors in the area.

Said to be an honest and upright man, he was deeply religious and founded the first Sunday school in the United States in Pawtucket. Joined in 1803 with his brother John Slater, they built the business to such a point that they established other mills, among them the Webster Mills, which were founded in 1812 in Webster, Massachusetts. During the War of 1812, the Slater Mills produced textiles that decreased the reliance on British imports. So successful was this mill that the United States government commissioned him to provide cloth for both the army and navy, which led him to being called the "Father of American manufacturers" by Andrew Jackson, president of the United States, when he visited him. Upon his death in 1835, Samuel Slater was perceived as a great business entrepreneur. He was succeeded by his son, Horatio Nelson Slater, who it was said "managed the business, developing it with rapidity and solidity" for forty-five years until his retirement in 1888, after which the business was trebled in volume under the direction of his nephew and adopted son Horatio Nelson Slater II. As one of many textile mills in the United States, great competition ensued, but by the late nineteenth century, after more than a century of steady growth, Slater had control of a major business concern.

Horatio Nelson Slater was married in 1891 to Mabel deC. Hunt of Boston and Milton, daughter of the famous artist William Morris Hunt, at Mizzentop, the Hunt family's summer house in Bar Harbor, Maine. (This was Slater's second marriage, as in 1858 he had married Elizabeth Vinton and had two children from that marriage, Caroline (Mrs. Charles G. Washburn) and Samuel Slater II.) Her mother, Louisa Dumaresq Perkins Hunt, was the daughter of Thomas Handasyd Perkins, the "Merchant Prince of Boston" and benefactor of both the Boston Athenaeum, to which he donated his Boston mansion as headquarters, and the Perkins Institution for the Blind, which was named in his honor. Slater, though wealthy in his own right, greatly benefited by his wife's relation to Boston Society, and they moved in a wealthy circle of friends. He donated the funds for Slater Hall, located on the College Green, at Brown University and was generous to charities throughout the United States.

The Slaters kept a town house at 448 Beacon Street in Boston's Back Bay and later purchased fifty-six acres of land from her family in Milton. Slater

The lodge on the Slater Estate, Pine Bank, had a large carriage house, horse stalls, tack room and a coachman's residence. *Author's collection.*

died in 1899 and was buried in the Slater Lot at Mount Zion Cemetery in Webster, where since 1812 there were Slater Mills. After his death, his widow had her brother, Paul Hunt, design a large rambling Tudor Revival mansion set on a knoll overlooking the extensive landscaped grounds that ran from Blue Hill Avenue to Brush Hill Road. Christening the estate Pine Bank, Mrs. Slater hired the Boston Symphony Orchestra to perform at her housewarming, according to her nephew, the late William Morris Hunt II. The Slater Mansion was sited on a knoll overlooking the circular carriage drive. The forecourt had a stone balustrade that overlooked the gardens and rustic twig-branch benches set throughout the grounds.

The Slaters summered at Pine Bank until the 1920s, when the estate was sold and became Jeanne d'Arc Academy, a Roman Catholic boarding and day school for girls. Mrs. Slater kept an apartment on Fifth Avenue in New York and died in 1942. Today, the Hunt-Slater Estate is part of the attractive campus of Curry College, and Pine Bank is used as a dormitory, albeit a magnificent one.

AMELIA PEABODY TILESTON

Amelia Tileston was a tireless worker for the relief of the poor and unfortunate of Serbia during and following World War I. Born and raised as the daughter of an affluent Milton family, she disdained pretense and went abroad during the war, serving as a nurse, canteen worker and general helper in Serbia until ill health took her life in 1920.

Amelia Peabody Tileston (1872–1920) was born at her paternal grandfather's mansion on Washington Street near Four Corners in Dorchester, the daughter of John Boies Tileston and Mary Wilder Foote Tileston. Her paternal grandfather was Edmund Pitt Tileston (1805–1873) of Dorchester, who inherited his father's share in the Tileston & Hollingsworth Paper Company on the Neponset River, which had been founded by Edmund Tileston and Mark Hollingsworth. Her parents had seven children, and after a brief sojourn in Concord and Brookline, they moved to Milton in 1889 and built Briarfield, designed by William Ralph Emerson. Amelia Tileston was educated at Milton Academy and St. Agnes' School in New York and was finished at Miss Folsom's School in Boston's Back Bay. Reputedly a bright, witty young lady, she was ever curious and took the obligatory grand

Amelia Peabody Tileston (1872–1920) was a tireless worker for the relief of the poor and unfortunate of Serbia during World War I. She was unflagging in her charitable acts, from walking dogs for the Animal Rescue League and studying nursing in South Boston and Roxbury to volunteering at day camps for tubercular patients where she "created an atmosphere of rest and cheer." *Author's collection.*

tour of Europe in 1895, later often traveling annually to the Continent. A friend at this time described her in the following way: "Her personality was striking and her charm rare. With what may be called a wealth of golden hair, daintily piquant features, clear blue eyes, and delicate coloring, she was a vivid figure that drew all eyes. Gifted with unusual vigor of body and mind, her expression was always alert and challenging, and her wit lighted up every conversation in which she shared."

Close to her mother and sisters following the death of John Boies Tileston in 1898, she went abroad with them for a year; upon her return to this country in 1899, she lived in Boston's Back Bay, summering in Milton until she moved here year round in the autumn of 1907. Her life was directed at doing such charitable acts as walking unadoptable dogs from the Animal Rescue League, studying nursing in the Roxbury and South Boston neighborhoods of Boston and working at day camps for tubercular patients. Her interest in tuberculosis was furthered by her involvement with the Boston Association for the Relief and Control of Tuberculosis, which operated a camp on Parker Hill (now the site of the New England Baptist Hospital) in Roxbury, an elevation thought beneficial for the cure of the disease. With "her kindly interest, ready sympathy, and quiet courage," she did much to cheer and comfort the patients under the care of Dr. David Townsend. A regular visitor, never arriving without gifts for the patients, she had "great sympathy and genuine interest in the welfare of the patients, especially the children, created an atmosphere of rest and cheer which aided much in their recuperation."

Following the death of her sister Eleanor Tileston, she went to New Haven, Connecticut, where she did social work at the New Haven General Hospital; upon the beginning of World War I in August 1914, she left in October for England, where she worked as a nurse in the Anglo-American Hospital in Paignton, Devonshire. Ever mindful of the fact that the United States still had not entered World War I, Miss Tileston's sense of duty was a prime example of someone who cared about the injured, sick and dying, regardless of their nationality or her country's involvement in a world war. Later, she did work for Belgian refugees in London and Paris; she eventually went to Italy, Serbia, Greece, India and Japan, offering her services wherever needed. She returned to Boston in 1915, remaining until the spring of 1916, when she sailed for Europe. She eventually reached Serbia, where she established a dressing station for the wounded and a canteen for soldiers. Having realized the great suffering of both adults as well as children, she also ran the Children's Fresh Air Camp at Avala, Serbia; her canteen for the Serbs assisted soldiers returning from the war. Her canteen in Belgrade provided the barest of comforts for the seven hundred or so soldiers who stopped in daily before their trains went to the front, and when she had them, she distributed warm clothing, blankets and cigarettes to them.

Working both day and night, she somehow found time to correspond with her mother, her sister Edith Tileston Eustis and her brother Wilder Tileston. However, when she developed pneumonia in February 1920, her heart was weakened, and she died shortly thereafter at the Scottish Women's Hospital. She was buried in Belgrade, at her request, in a plot donated by the municipality in tribute to her work for Serbia, and where "her grave...will continually recall her to the memory of those whom she loved and served so devotedly."

WORLD WAR I VETERANS

Joyce Ford of the Milton Selectmen's Office called me in regards to a short article she read in *Reminiscence Magazine* that questioned the origin of a World War I medal that was given to veterans of the Great War from Milton. The circular bronze medal has a soaring eagle surmounting the town seal with the words "World War Service" along the edge; the reverse has the words "Presented to her gallant sons by the Town of Milton in grateful recognition of their part in the World War 1917–1918." This medal, which was originally suspended from a silk ribbon, was given to our fellow townsmen who served in the Allied cause. Well, Ms. Ford actually sent me on an enjoyable task, which was to find out about these medals and what they actually represented, which I hope will answer her interesting question. According to the *Milton Record*, the town held a "Welcome Home Day" on Saturday, October 11, 1919, for the six-hundred-plus men and women who served in World War I. The daylong event had the servicemen and nurses gathered at the festively decorated and bunting bedecked Milton Town Hall, where it was said that "officers and privates rubbed elbows in the ranks and soldiers and sailors fraternized with the best of good spirits."

The selectmen led the cordial welcome and proffered the sincere thanks of their fellow townsmen and townswomen to the soldiers, sailors and nurses for their duty to their country and their community. Following the gathering at 2:00 p.m., the veterans formed a parade under the direction of the officers of the Milton Post, American Legion, and the accompanying music was provided by the Ives Military Band as the parade left town hall and proceeded along White Street (now Reedsdale Road) and Brook Road, where they gathered at the Brook Road (now Kelly) Playground. Here a baseball game was played by the army versus navy. A tug-of-war, a tilting match, obstacle and sack races and a band concert also took place.

At 4:45 p.m., there was a presentation of medals to "All those Milton residents who went to war," with a brief address by Maurice A. Duffy, chairman of the selectmen, in front of town hall. The selectmen and members of the committee stood on the steps of town hall as 347 soldiers, sailors and nurses approached Mr. Duffy and were pinned with this bronze medal. The newspaper recorded that the great "majority were in the uniform of the United States Army, Navy, Marine Corps and Aviation Corps, but there were four women in nurses' uniforms." For the 25 men who did not return, having given their lives as the supreme sacrifice in the defense of

In Flanders Field was designed by renowned artist Daniel Chester French (1850–1931). The Town of Milton commissioned this bronze monument for "the 25 men who did not return, having given their lives as the supreme sacrifice in defense of their country" during World War I. It stands on a lawn between the Milton Town Hall and the First Congregational Church. *Author's collection.*

their country, "Taps" was played in remembrance, and the singing of the "Star-Spangled Banner" accompanied the raising of the flag. A supper was held in an illuminated and decorated tent in the rear of town hall for the servicemen and guests, in addition to the welcoming committee, which numbered 1,000 people. The supper was followed by a band concert and fireworks, and dancing to the Ives Orchestra was held in town hall.

Today the most prominent memorial to World War I in Milton is the impressive bronze statue *In Flanders Field* by Daniel Chester French near the drive to town hall facing Canton Avenue, but these few hundred bronze medals, thanks to Joyce Ford, are remembered in Milton over eight decades later, and we remember the Allied cause and what our fellow townsmen sacrificed for us.

In his stirring poem "We Shall Not Sleep," Dr. John McCrae commemorated the men of World War I who gave the supreme sacrifice:

In Flanders fields the poppies blow
Between the crosses; row on row,
That mark our place; and in the sky
The larks still bravely singing fly,
Scarce heard amidst the guns below.

We are the dead.
Short days ago we lived, felt dawn, saw sunset glow,
Loved and were loved.
And now we lie in Flanders fields.

Take up our quarrel with the foe,
To you from failing hands we throw the torch,
Be yours to hold it high; if ye break faith with us who die,
We shall not sleep, though poppies grow
In Flanders field.

W. CAMERON FORBES

W. Cameron Forbes (1870–1959) was the son of William Hathaway and Edith Emerson Forbes of Milton Hill and grandson of the great railroad magnate John Murray Forbes of Fredonia in Milton and the transcendentalist writer Ralph Waldo Emerson of Concord. Graduated from Harvard in 1892, where he also served as head coach for the "Varsity Eleven" under Captain Cabot (1897) and Captain Dibblee (1898), he played substitute end rush on the football team. Associated with the Boston engineering firm of Stone & Webster following his graduation, he was involved in the management of electrical properties throughout the United States, acting as president of a number of these corporations. He was also a partner of Forbes & Company, a family concern, and a trustee of the Baker Chocolate Company.

Appointed governor general of the Philippines in 1908, he served with great éclat for five years in the development of the different resources of the country, such as hemp, sugar, tobacco, coconut oil, rubber and gutta-percha.

Manila, a corruption of the name *may nilad*—meaning "profuse with nilad," a small white flower—is a cultural blend of East and West. The people of the Philippines, primarily Tagalogs and Cebuanos, affectionately called him "Caminero" Forbes, as one resident said, "because he was responsible for the beginning of our wonderful road system here in the Philippines." In addition to good roads, he worked for good railroads, good harbors and a sound economy. Forbes lived at Malacanang, the official residence of the governors general in Manila. Derived from the phrase *May lakan diyan*, which means "there are nobles in that place," Manila, which had been under Spanish rule since it was claimed in 1521 by Ferdinand Magellan for Spain, would be the Philippine Republic until it became United States territory in 1898. Following his return to the United States, Forbes was appointed United States ambassador to Japan in 1930 and also served on the Council on Foreign Relations.

John Murray Forbes had in 1843 bought an interest and in 1856 purchased Naushon Island, often called "Queen the Elizabeth Islands," from William W. Swain, his wife's uncle, where he built the Stone House. The island is still a rural retreat owned by the Forbes family and is only accessible by boat from Woods Hole. Here Cameron Forbes, John Murray Forbes's grandson, sailed *Onawa*, his seventy-foot, twelve-meter yacht designed by W. Starling Burgess and built in 1928 by Abeking & Rasmussen. Forbes also kept the two-hundred-acre Gay Farm in Ellis, part of Norwood, Massachusetts, a ranch in Wyoming and Birdwood Plantation, his winter home in Thomasville, Georgia, which is now Thomas University.

The visit of Calvin Coolidge (1872–1933) to Naushon was obviously a great honor. Born in Plymouth Notch, Vermont, he was a graduate of Amherst College and practiced law before he became governor of Massachusetts. He served as the thirtieth president of the United States from 1923 to 1929 as a conservative, distinguished and well-respected man who restored "the dignity and prestige of the Presidency when it had reached the lowest ebb in our history...in a time of extravagance and waste." A true Yankee with a dry acerbic wit, he is still often remembered for some of his *bon mots* and quotes, such as, "Collecting more taxes than is absolutely necessary is legalized robbery," "One with the law is a majority" and, "The right thing to do never requires any subterfuge, it is always simple and direct." Though his family home in Vermont is open as a museum, his presidential library was established in 1920 in a memorial room in the Forbes Library in Northampton, Massachusetts, which was built from a bequest of Judge Charles Forbes.

After his death in 1958, Cameron Forbes was buried in the Forbes Lot at Milton Cemetery, alongside his father, William Hathaway Forbes, who was the first president of what would become the American Telephone & Telegraph Company—two men who made tremendous contributions to the fabric of American life.

DR. MATTHEW VASSAR PIERCE

Dr. Matthew Vassar Pierce (1855–1937) was a noted and well-respected physician in Milton from 1882 until his death in 1937. Perceived as unassuming, reassuring and diligent in his ministering to the ill in town, he was said to have become "a much loved doctor here until his death." The son of Samuel Stillman and Ellen M.T. Wallis Pierce, Dr. Pierce was born on Green Street in the West End of Boston, where his father kept S.S. Pierce & Company, a noted purveyor of gourmet foods and fine liquors, at the corner of Tremont and Court Streets. The Pierces also kept a summer house on Marsh Street (now Gallivan Boulevard) east of Granite Avenue in Dorchester near their ancestral home, the Robert and Ann Grenaway Pierce House, which was built circa 1650 and still stands on Oakton Avenue. A graduate of Harvard College, Dr. Pierce later matriculated at the Harvard Medical School, graduating in 1880. Upon his graduation, he was married to Margaret Gray Whitten, daughter of Alderman Charles V. Whitten of Dorchester, and they sailed for Europe, where Dr. Pierce continued his medical studies at clinics and hospitals in Berlin, Heidelberg and Vienna.

The Pierces returned to Boston in 1882 and purchased a four-acre tract of land in Milton, bounded by Canton Avenue, Centre Street and Vose's Lane. They contracted with local builder Frederick M. Severance to build a large gambrel-roofed Colonial Revival house, which was completed in 1883 (now 414 Canton Avenue). The Pierce House and the Whitney House (known as Elm Corner) were the only houses on this triangular tract of land until the Roberts House was built in 1893 at 70 Centre Street, and they would remain so until the mid-twentieth century, when developed by William Crosby. Here the Pierces lived for the next five decades, raising a family of four children. Beginning in 1882, Dr. Pierce's "skill gained for him an enormous obstetric

Dr. Matthew Vassar Pierce (1855–1937) was a beloved and well-respected physician in Milton for over fifty years. In 1903, he founded the Milton Convalescent Home, which was the forerunner of the Milton Hospital, of which he served as chief of staff for three decades. He was said to have carried "comfort, skilled care, unfailing kindness, sympathy and understanding to practically every member of town, at one time or another." *Courtesy of Frances Pierce Field.*

practice, most of which was accomplished in the homes of his patients." One of his numerous deliveries was Miss Virginia Holbrook (1899–2000), who was the daughter of Ridgeway and Eleanora Holbrook and was delivered by Dr. Pierce at the family home on Randolph Avenue. She would eventually live during three centuries.

In 1903, Dr. Pierce founded the Milton Convalescent Home, the predecessor to the present Milton Hospital. This was a full-time home that was related to Miss Ware's Convalescents' Home on Canton Avenue, which was only in operation during the summer months. The new home saw increased services in 1905 to include hospital facilities, as well as a convalescence home, of which he served as chief of staff for the next thirty-one years. The facility was located in the old Cunningham Mansion that had been built in 1871 by Edward Cunningham. The 150-acre estate was purchased by the Cunningham Foundation, established in 1904 by Mary Abbot Forbes

A nurse greets two women seated in an inglenook at the Milton Hospital, the former mansion of Edward and Frances Cary Cunningham. Used until 1950 as Milton Hospital, it served a growing population that by mid-century truly needed a modern institution. *Courtesy of Milton Hospital.*

Cunningham (1814–1904) and used as the Convalescent Home until 1950, along with other recreational benefits for Milton residents. The Convalescent Home grew in its medical services to the town and was once said to be "a monument to his charitable enterprise." He was a founder of the Milton Savings Bank, a director of S.S. Pierce & Company and a member of the Dorchester Medical Club, which was "his constant love, to which, as was usual with him, he gave much more than he could have possibly received." A modest man in regards to his numerous accomplishments, he initially traveled to his patients throughout Milton by a horse-drawn two-wheeled gig, which was later replaced by an automobile with the license plate 4249. Well known in Milton for five decades, it was said that he "carried comfort, skilled care, unfailing kindness, sympathy and understanding to practically every member of town, at one time or another."

DR. TUDOR AND LICENSE PLATE NO. 1

It's interesting that the Registry of Motor Vehicles offers an annual lottery of low-number license plates, which is dutifully subscribed by thousands of Massachusetts residents hoping to receive a coveted low license plate. Of course, a five-number license plate is adequate but decidedly middle class when compared with a four-number plate. However, should one have a three- or two-digit number or, the most coveted, a single-number license plate, nirvana is actually said to have been achieved. I knew one person who had two sequential three-number license plates that were inherited from his grandfather, who actually salivated over a single-digit plate as the car passed him on the highway; it was at that point I realized that the penchant for this status symbol was far more endemic and more wholeheartedly ascribed to than I wanted to allow myself to believe.

The license plate in Massachusetts was devised due to the efforts of Major Henry Lee Higginson (1834–1919), who is called the "Father of the American License Plate" and the "First Citizen of Boston." Higginson was a wealthy financier who lived with his wife, Ida Agassiz Higginson, at 274 Beacon Street in Boston's Back Bay, which was designed by H.H. Richardson, who later commissioned Rand & Whitney to design the Hotel Agassiz, a residential apartment house at 191 Commonwealth Avenue in Boston's Back Bay where the Higginsons later lived. Higginson was the president of the Boston Symphony Orchestra and for two decades personally funded the symphony. He was the promoter of the McKim, Mead and White building constructed in 1900 at Massachusetts and Huntington Avenues in the Back Bay Fens. As a prominent banker and philanthropist, Higginson was to secure the future of the symphony and ensure its success, but it was the speeding motorists of the new "horseless carriages" near his summer estate, Sunset Hill, in Manchester by the Sea, that caused his chagrin. It was said that there were numerous complaints about the rudeness of the unlicensed automobile enthusiasts, and there was no way to regulate them or identify the offending drivers. Higginson, on the road outside his estate, "arranged to set up an elaborate network of timing devises in order to prove that over half the town's motor traffic was routinely exceeding the speed limit of 15 miles per hour." The only problem was how to identify the culprits, so Higginson submitted a petition to the Massachusetts legislature in 1903 about this problem, which was entitled *A Petition Relative to Licensing Automobiles and Those Operating the Same*.

With his wide sphere of influence and great respect, Higginson's petition was received with acclaim and voted into law; by June 1903, licenses were issued to those owning automobiles in Massachusetts, and so began the first instance of state-issued license plates in the United States.

The new license plates were made of high-gloss porcelain enamel and bore the title "Massachusetts Automobile Register" and a number, which henceforth was kept by a new state agency, the Registry of Motor Vehicles. This allowed owners of automobiles to be licensed, registered and identified for traffic infractions. License plate No. 1 (as well as No. 99) was issued to Frederic Tudor (1869–1939), a nephew of Ida and Henry Higginson, and it is still registered to a descendant. Tudor was working with Massachusetts state highway officials at that time, but it is not recorded if this license was a case of favoritism or if he happened to be the first to register his automobiles. Whatever the reason was, by 1907 there were over twenty-four thousand licenses issued, and a year later the enamel license plates were redesigned and were required, by law, to be mounted on the front and the rear of each automobile. By this time, numbers had exceeded single-, double-, triple- and even quadruple-digit license plate numbers, and the exclusivity of these

The home of Dr. Frederick Tudor is at 51 Randolph Avenue, an elegant Greek Revival house built about 1830 by Robert Todd, a lumber dealer in Milton Village. *Author's collection.*

early license plates became a sense of pride and a coveted family holding to be passed down. It was not until 1911 that the "reserve system" concerning license plates was put into effect so that "anyone with a license plate number below 5000 [could]...keep that number automatically upon re-registration or to transfer it to a relative."

Frederic and Amy Logan Tudor lived on River Street on the flat of Beacon Hill and kept a comfortable weekend house in Sandwich. The Tudors descended from Frederic Tudor, known as the "Ice King of Boston" due to his uniquely adroit marketing skills in the shipment of ice to warm-climate locations, where it was then sold to inhabitants for astronomical sums of money. One of his grandsons, Frederic Tudor, built the Tudor on Mount Vernon Street, which was a fashionable apartment house where his widow, Louise Simes Tudor, lived until her death in 1934. Their son was Frederic Tudor, and he and his wife eventually had the prestigious license plate No. 1 transferred to them. The Tudors retained the coveted license plate until it was transferred in 1940 to their son, Dr. Frederic Tudor (1907–1985), and his wife, Mary Allerton Cushman Tudor. Though both had been raised on Beacon Hill (Mary Tudor was the daughter of Robert and Mary Poland Cushman of 98 Mount Vernon Street), they purchased 51 Randolph Avenue in 1946 after the death of Mrs. Stevens. The house was built about 1830 by Robert McIlvaine Todd (1802–1890), a lumber dealer in Milton Village, and is a perfect example of a Greek Revival cottage with four fluted Doric columns supporting an overhanging roof. Dr. Tudor was associated with the Milton Convalescent Home and eventually become the respected chief of staff of the Milton Hospital. The Tudors became active members of the community, and here they raised their children, Mary Tudor (Mrs. George Allen Holloway) and Robert Tudor. Following Dr. Tudor's death in 1985, the coveted license plate was transferred to his son, who though a resident of Chicago, retains the license plate, which is affixed to an automobile that today lives in a Beacon Hill garage.

HANNAH GILBERT PALFREY AYER

Hannah Ayer moved and had the Suffolk Resolves House restored in 1950. Once located in Milton Village (the present site of the Citizens Bank), the house was slated for demolition, but she was determined to save this historic house and move it to a corner of her estate on Canton Avenue in Milton

Hannah Palfrey Ayer and Dr. James Bourne Ayer saved the Suffolk Resolves House in 1950 by having it moved to a corner of their estate on Canton Avenue. Their generosity in saving this historic house and their donation in 1963 to the Milton Historical Society has ensured an enduring legacy. *Courtesy of Tally Saltonstall Forbes.*

to ensure the preservation of what has been called the "Birthplace of the American Revolution." Mrs. Ayer was a multifaceted woman, known to be dutiful, conscientious, erudite and all that was expected of a woman of her background, and this restoration of a historic house created an important contribution and ensuring legacy to local history.

Hannah Gilbert Palfrey (1888–1963) was the daughter of General John Carver and Adelaide E. Payson Palfrey and was born in Belmont. John C. Palfrey (1833–1906) was a military engineer in the Civil War and a wealthy textile manufacturer in Lowell, Massachusetts. Among her noted ancestors was Colonel William Palfrey, aide-de-camp of George Washington during the Revolution and paymaster general of the army; he was appointed consul general to France, where he was lost at sea sailing to his appointment in 1780. Her grandfather was the Reverend John Gorham Palfrey, a noted Unitarian minister in Boston and author of the *History of New England to the Revolutionary War*, in five volumes, of which the first appeared in 1859 and the last posthumously in 1890. Reverend Palfrey was minister of the Brattle Square Church from 1818 to 1831, later serving as professor of Biblical literature and dean of faculty at the Harvard Divinity School.

The Palfrey family moved from Belmont to 88 Beacon Street in Boston's Back Bay, and Hannah Palfrey attended Miss Winsor's School and later the Garland School of Homemaking. After completing her education, she served as a kindergarten teacher for underprivileged children and later at the first Montessori School in Boston. Her marriage in 1909 to Dr. James Bourne Ayer (1882–1963), a graduate of Harvard in 1903 and the Harvard Medical School, was an enduring and mutually supportive one. Dr. Ayer was the James Jackson Putnam Professor of Neurology at Harvard Medical School and chief of neurology at Massachusetts General Hospital. He was a practicing physician in Boston and a member of several medical associations, including the Boston Society for Medical Improvement, the Obstetrical Society of Boston, the Massachusetts Medical Society and the American Medical Society.

The Ayers initially lived at 25 Lime Street on the flat of Beacon Hill but moved to Milton Village when their children were young. At a later date, they purchased a large estate at 1350 Canton Avenue in Milton, where they created impressive gardens that were tended by Dr. Ayer and their gardener, Charles Carveth, who with his wife, Edith B. Carveth, lived in the Suffolk Resolves House. The Ayer house at 1350 Canton Avenue had been built circa 1780 by Dr. John Sprague (1754–1800), who was one of the earliest physicians in Milton, having studied medicine with his father and in Europe. Originally, the house was on the present site of the Suffolk Resolves House, but it was moved to the crest of the hill by the Eustis family. The estate had an expansive mansion that had sufficient room for the Ayer family, as they had six children: Hannah (known as Nancy), Susannah Cazneau, Mary (known as Molly) Farwell, Elizabeth, James B. Ayer Jr. and John Palfrey Ayer.

Fully supporting her husband in his career, Hannah Ayer was to devote herself to historical pursuits after her children had become adults, becoming a "noted antiquarian and historian." She was proud of the fact that her grandfather had served in the American Revolution under Washington.

Mrs. Ayer served as the editor of the book *A Brief History of Milton Massachusetts* and was editor in 1950 of *A Legacy of New England, Letters of the Palfrey Family*. A member of the Massachusetts Historical Society, she served as president of the Milton Historical Society and as a trustee of the Society for the Preservation of New England Antiquities (now Historic New England). A great clubwoman, she was a member of the Parliamentary Law Club, the Warren and Prescott Chapter, Daughters of the American Revolution, the Chilton Club and the Nucleus Club.

However, it was her interest and determination to save the Suffolk Resolves House that has ensured an enduring legacy. With the assistance of William Morris Hunt II, her "architect-engineer" and fellow board member of the Milton Historical Society, the house was saved from

The Suffolk Resolves House was on Adams Street in Milton Village, to the left of the Associates Building. Once the home of Daniel and Rachel Smith Vose, it was adapted for commercial purposes by the late nineteenth century. The house was saved by Hannah Ayer when she had it moved in 1950 to a corner of her estate on Canton Avenue in Milton. *Author's collection.*

demolition and moved to a corner of her Milton estate, where it was restored and made comfortable for her gardener and his wife, who lived on the second floor. Mrs. Ayer set about restoring the house to its mid-eighteenth-century appearance. Once two distinct houses, the right part dating from the late seventeenth century and the left to circa 1765, they had been joined in 1785. Hunt placed the historic house on a knoll overlooking Canton Avenue, and Mrs. Ayer selected wallpapers and historic paint colors for the interior, taking courses on the painting of fireplace tiles and dyeing crimson her grandmother Palfrey's enormous damask tablecloths for window swags. A preservationist and knowledgeable decorative arts patron, she studied tile designs at Colonial Williamsburg and painted the dining room tiles. She recreated the home of Daniel and Rachel Smith Vose, opening it to schoolchildren and the interested public on special occasions. Upon her death, she bequeathed the Suffolk Resolves House to the Milton Historical Society, which has maintained her vision for almost five decades.

As the white marble plaque on the façade of the Suffolk Resolves states:

In this Mansion
On the Ninth Day of September 1774 at a meeting of the delegates of
Every Town and District in the County of Suffolk, the
Suffolk Resolves were adopted.

"Posterity will acknowledge that virtue which preserved them free and happy." Well, Hannah G.P. Ayer also deserves our accolades and the recognition of her fellow Miltonians, in that she preserved the historic house where the Suffolk Resolves were signed before being taken by horseback by Paul Revere to Philadelphia, where they were approved by the Continental Congress.

Jeannette Lithgow Peverly

De mortuis nil nisi bonum. ("Of the dead [say] nothing but good.") It's a respectful adage that the poet Quintus Horatius Flaccus (known as Horace) recited over two thousand years ago, yet in regards to Jeannette Peverly, it was something that only good *could* be said. With her death in September

2009, she is mourned not just by her family but also by a legion of friends who cherished her friendship and sought her company.

Jeannette Lithgow Peverly (1914–2009) was the daughter of Arthur Washington and Ina Berenice Robinson Lithgow and was born in Puerto Plata, Dominican Republic. The Lithgows were second-generation sugar planters in the Dominican Republic and, in the early twentieth century, were the proprietors of an electric utility company. The family was prominent, and her entrepreneurial father would serve as United States consul to the Dominican Republic. In 1916, the family returned to Boston and settled in Melrose, Massachusetts, where she was educated. Her marriage to Russell Peverly was a mutually supportive and enduring one, and after their move to Milton in 1939, they joined the First Parish Church Unitarian and began volunteerism that would last until their deaths. Indeed, as the Reverend Jeffrey

Jeannette Lithgow Peverly (1914–2009) was said to have been "part of the backbone of everything she was involved in." A longtime member of the Milton Historical Society, the Forbes House Museum, the Milton Woman's Club and the Boston Home, she was a mainstay and beloved participant in every worthy cause. Awarded in 2008 the "Thanks for Giving" award by the Milton Interfaith Clergy Association, her many years of ecumenical spirit were both recognized and embraced. *Photo by Edith G. Clifford*

Johnson said of her, Jeannette "was part of the backbone of everything she was involved in."

Raising three daughters—Martha Lewis, Ellen McCarran and Joanne Pedro—the Peverlys always found time to share and participate in community events, among them Jeannette serving as a neighborhood warden during World War II, ensuring that blackout shades were in place at dusk. Jeannette was to serve as the church secretary at the First Parish Church under the Reverend Dr. Prescott Browning Wintersteen and as a librarian at the Milton Public Library. As a member of the Milton Woman's Club and the Forbes House Museum, where she also served as a docent, her interest in all aspects of history was evident. In fact, she was the historian of the First Parish Church, where her vivid memory, unbounded enthusiasm and life experiences linked generations of Miltonians. As a trustee of the Boston Home in Dorchester, she continued her volunteerism, making residents of the home as comfortable and content as possible.

About a decade ago, a large boulder was placed on a large open field on the east side of Sumner Street. Simply engraved "Peverly Park," it was placed there by one who remembered Russell and Jeannette Peverly and their interest and concern for the children of the neighborhood. Nothing could have been more appropriate, as this solid rock co-memorializes a woman whose steadfast and abiding desire was to always do good.

However, it was her involvement with the Milton Historical Society that seemed to give her the greatest pleasure. She and her husband were among the members with the longest membership, and they were mainstays at every event at the Suffolk Resolves House or at lectures held at various locations throughout town. As hostess at society events, she laid a lovely table and always served her famous "sherry squares," which were delicious treats but became increasingly potent as time went on. Her daughter, Joanne Pedro, brought a tray of these sherry squares to the Suffolk Resolves Open House last October, and they were enjoyed by all not just for their deliciousness but also for the memory they evoked.

Jeannette Peverly never missed the fifth-grade tours of the Milton Public Schools that were held in the late spring. She greeted the enthusiastic students and showed them not just the First Parish Church but also the Children's Church. Lucky was the student who got to ring the bell exiting the Children's Church after a historical lecture. Her sense of pride in being a Miltonian was evident, and she also reveled in reading and learning and volunteered in the Milton Room at the library on Saturday mornings for years. She was generous with her time, helpful, energetic and truly seemed interested in everyone's special research project. In 2008, the First Parish Church nominated her to receive the "Thanks for Giving" award, which is given annually by the Milton Interfaith Clergy Association, of which she was an ardent supporter. The award recognized this woman and her many years of ecumenical spirit.

Shortly before her death, as she was visited by family and friends, she asked me the date of the open house in October in recognition of the Suffolk Resolves. When told the date, she smiled and said, "I'll be there." Her death the next day was sudden, but on the day of the open house, she really was with us, and as we shared her "sherry squares" we remembered a well-loved friend.

ABOUT THE AUTHOR

Anthony Sammarco is a noted historian and author of fifty-seven books on the history and development of Boston. He commenced writing for Arcadia Publications in 1995, and among his books, *Dorchester* made the *Boston Globe*'s Bestseller's List and has gone through numerous reprints. *Boston's Back Bay in the Victorian Era, Boston's West End, Boston's South End, Boston's North End* (and *Il North End di Boston*, in Italian) and *The Great Boston*

Fire of 1872 are among his bestselling books. His three local books—*Milton Then & Now* (2004) and the co-authored books with the late Paul Buchanan, *Milton* and *Milton Architecture*—have been widely acclaimed.

Mr. Sammarco has taught history at the Urban College of Boston since 1996, where he was named educator of the year in 2003 and where he serves on the Leadership Council. His course, "Boston's Immigrants," was developed especially for the Urban College and its diverse student base, and his book *Boston's Immigrants* was written to highlight the diversity of the city. He has received the Bulfinch Award from the Doric Dames of the Massachusetts State House and the Washington Medal from Freedom Foundation for his work in history. He was elected a Fellow of the Massachusetts Historical Society, is a member of the Boston Author's Club and the Massachusetts Charitable Mechanics Association and is a proprietor of the Boston Athenaeum. In his volunteer work, he is treasurer of the Victorian Society, New England Chapter, chair of the trustees of the Milton Cemetery, trustee of the Forest Hills Cemetery Educational Trust, board member and curator of the Milton Historical Society and a trustee of the Captain Forbes House Museum; he is also a Milton Town Meeting member from Precinct 5. He is past president of the Bay State Historical League and the Dorchester Historical Society, a former trustee and treasurer of the Milton Public Library, a past member of the Milton Historical Commission and has served as a corporator of the New England Baptist Hospital for a decade.